WORLD LITERATURE
IN TRANSLATION

CHANTAL CHAWAF

MOTHER LOVE,
MOTHER EARTH

Translated from the French with an Afterword by
MONIQUE FLEURY NAGEM

GARLAND PUBLISHING, INC.
NEW YORK & LONDON 1992

Library of Congress Cataloging-in-Publication Data
Chawaf, Chantal.
    [Retable. English]
    Mother love ; Mother earth / Chantal Chawaf ; translated with an
afterword by Monique Nagem.
        p. cm. — (World literature in translation ; v. 20)
    Translation of: Retable ; La rêverie.
    ISBN 0-8240-4399-5
    I. Chawaf, Chantal. Rêverie. English. 1990. II. Title. III. Title:
Mother earth. IV. Series: Garland library world literature in translation ; v.
20.
PQ2663.H379R413   1990
843'.914—dc20   90-3034

Printed on acid-free, 250-year-life paper
Manufactured in the United States of America

MOTHER LOVE,
MOTHER EARTH

MOTHER LOVE

I. *Birth*

Cornute, the milky grass spatters, sparkles, carts in its green current, hairs, feathers, seeds, nails, intertwining fins, all furrowed by the membrane, the lining, the batter, entrail wool, fertile, lunar behind the oaks, behind the chestnut trees. The debris, the mucus moisten the air, the little one moves, the child like the wailing call of an ailing adult, like the shivering of getting to bed, lank, in the fetal position, under the dome of the skull, at the site of the lesion. Nations crush each other with their jaws, like meat in their mouth. Gestures crush, break, strike, dislocate, cover with helmets, mobilize, above black clumps. Emitted by the sun, streets without water, in the abandoned reservoir, drain even the cavities whose torn organs wander. Rocks hit, whip, roll, lash, occluding sun, bullets, collide with the dead soldiers. Splinter, wither, rupture the branches. Slit of the mouth, orbit, absorbed in the pool spurted out like a beard of sweet and sticky juice thick as the childhood excreted by the grass coffins. A cross of bones clenches, crackles on the raw bottom of the blows on the clouds. In acrid waves, of both lungs, the dead child skimmed, doubled up as a nest, as a rattle, begins to flow. Cuttlefish, octopus pole, gills, caterpillar, we descend, carbon without vertebrae, without crest, detached from the black, carnal rocks into which the thrust empties itself, the contour of the puncture pinches, fascinates, confronted with the jelly of the child, unable to ford the baby clothes of cereals and the wind from the plants, the air, expired, they scour, they convulse, sour with powdery spirals they search for the organs, to tear them, to drink their throbbing hair, to engulf, they rumble, to be lost there, each martyr huddles in his fear trembling, resisting, rolling toward explosions where to grow shatters on the crash.

Hard and cutting, the debris, hidden in me. I wander.

9

I would like to leave. I am afraid. I have nowhere to go. I would like to be far away. Somewhere else.

— What was she like?
— I saw her.
— You saw her?
— Taller than your mother.
— What was she like?
— Taller than your mother.
— What was she like?
— Blonde. She had class. Authoritarian look; she knew what she wanted.

To leave me—She walks through the hospital corridors—The light is gray—To leave me—A wartime light, a stormy summer light in Paris, a light of abandonment. Sky of Northern beaches, rows of wooden pickets. I play with my cousins near the bunkers. Watch out for the rusty torpedoes, the shells. I don't feel like going swimming, the water is dark. Several times already I have asked my mother.

—She was married.
"—She was not married. She seemed very sweet.
She had probably followed her family's wishes."
—She seemed sure of herself, strong. She was a woman who must have had affairs.
Or:
"—She was studying with him. He was older than she. He was married. She fell in love."
"—She was a student, I think. We tried to find out who she was."
But you do not know. Her blond hair, taller than your mother, she was from the North. I would like to ask more. I observe my father's defeated look.
—She said he was a math professor. She said what she wanted to. Maybe he was a garbage collector. Surely you are socially better off with us.

A woman's laughter, like a cawing, echoes through the empty courtyards.

I come out of the movie theater, relaxed, a little tired. It is night.

I feel my long legs, the movement of my hips. The mauve wool of my dress moulds my body. I meet, like brief lights, the eyes of strangers.

—Little girl, that is not called giving birth; it's called dropping like a cow. She did not even have the guts to have an abortion. I shiver.
—If she had had that kind of courage, I wouldn't be here.
—No.
Nine months of my life lived by her blond life. To protect, at all times, against death, against the degeneration of the future, a life denied; the tenderness of another will be nourished by the tenderness that I am forming with my blood, with the oranges that I eat, the milk that I drink, my fatigue, the sun where I stroll, I dream, I feel bitter, nine months during the war.

I look up: a wall. A wall above a wall. My head is tilted. I am below. The walls rise, rise.

I will never know her.

"Psh! you? a war turd they picked up because of the immoral women full of sex and fear."

What was it that was yellow, dilated, very open? Gaping? Maybe it was edged with liquid? It was lighted up. What?...blonde...but empty ... But I do not. I no longer have the strength to wait, standing; I sit. The black stain is expanding. I wait, huddled. No one comes.

Blonde and ash-blonde stains twirl, in the distance, numerous, they blondulate.

—It will be my first real joy in many years, this trip with you. Oh! Look! I should be laughing instead I'm crying. The streets, the canals of Venice, all that will be a nice change. I love you so tenderly. Do you remember when you used to say: "—A little kiss mommy"? You know you'll always be my own little one.

We'll be together. We'll go for walks, after all these years these days I lost denying her, wanting to replace her but I can still build it all, let myself be "her little girl." She is ready, adoptive. She'll be wearing her light muslin dress. How she will love the Veronese and the sun, through the windows, high up and the waters that move, that smell. Oh! I will weave her into that blondelette light, I will return the air and the wind to her; she will have the pink sun, and the sunny pink of the marble in her eyes. We will be completely surrounded by water.

This sweetness before dinner. The sex of the town between two cypresses. Stains. A blood stain.

Domes. We are near. Move. Where is my mother? The strands of my hair lash my face. We are drawwwwnnn . . . we are looosst—Heavy fingers on my shoulder like a slap. The wind discolors our lips and our eyes. Waves fall on our words. Us foam your ticket foam they scatstrecherize us. The floor goes up and down. Honeysuckle, paving stones, sun, the water. Snatches of pink empty snackbars, growing dim, the inside of a cafeteria, in a basement floor. Smell of gasoline during several hours of delay. Puffy cheeks in front of a ticket window. We are locked in. A blue semi-circle. The blue and gold mosaic of Saint-Mark's facade. The clock above Lulu's plaid skirt. We are seated next to each other along the wrought-iron finials.

"Kiddo! Kiddo! Shouts Lulu, kid of a kiddo!" My aunt's eyes are striped by the spaghetti hanging from my fork. Lido. Not the tourists in greenery and in orange but winter branches. Not the sea but the sky which recedes as we approach. My mother gets out of breath, stumbles, presses her body against mine. There is not even a movie house we can go into to rest just closed shops. Near me, my mother in her black coat, smiling, full of good will and concealed resentment. I persist. Maybe it's over there, over there white, empty, over there, maybe . . . My mother does not protest. How many avenues like this have we walked down without finding the beach nor the white building, and without hearing the voice near a brick church? While we keep on looking, the Palace of the Doges, the museums are closing, on the other side of the sea. My father, my aunt, and Lulu, feet in pigeons, cameras on their shoulders, must be looking for us and eating croissants among the columns. "—So, what in the world were you two doing? We looked for you everywhere! Eh! Ghyslaine, How about the Veronese women you promised me? That's not fair; you don't give a damn, you've been here before." The gray and the pink fly off, rise in a swirl, for an instant toward the blue without reaching it and alight on the ground. "—Shit, oh! shit! shit! shit!" Once more we are sitting down. We wait. My father searches. I shiver. We have not had lunch. We spend three hours a day prowling around the snack-bars, discussing prices, swallowing platefuls of spaghetti, waiting for the chocolate ice cream we ordered. Premonition. The whole maternity of the water nurses the light. Sparkles. Wings. Eyelashes. The parents chat, seated, behind the pineapples, the mayonnaise, the cigarettes, the purses. The road to San Remo where the Mediterranean roars; now Venice is no more than a passing fit of nerves, domes, breasts shameful: "—How she makes herself up I think it makes her eyes look . . . " Her face behind the car door. Heavy rain from Northern Italy. Clouds and land "—Good bye" "—Good bye" "—Goooodbyeee (my aunt) bye ye her hairy wrist, her hand (me) good bye, her hand behind the nape of her neck, touches, I lean over, squeeze Lulu's hand" "Ah! if only I didn't have my birthday to celebrate . . . " He is driving, stirs his body. The road is like fur. In the front my aunt laughs "—I would have made your girls dance to death!" Pff! Pff! Dyed bangs. Ahaah. Hysteria. Lulu keeps quiet. Her lips, red vulva in the dark. Curved roads. Electric lights. Reflections on the water. Hotel on a hill. If only I did not have my birthday to celebrate . . . Mine, her hips in the bedroom mirror. Rest you down dinner fresh. Spruce. Slow. Gray. Fissures. Little black circles which crawl over me, over my arms, over the bedspread. My mother kisses me. "Are you happy?" she asks, under the arcades, behind the Palace of the Doges, I think. Did I thank her? But I felt the black of her not so thick coat. For a few minutes my mother spoke louder, faster. She laughed, the laugh of a mother used to laughing with her real daughter.

"—Oh! Mamma! Oh, Mamma!" "—Oh!, mamma."

"—When we get home, if it will help, I promise to start looking for her." "—Maybe she's dead."

The water once more. The water which goes up and down, under us. Slanting bodies. Digestion. Lazy feeling. Starting of the engine. "Come, we'll take a walk like two big girls; let's leave those broads, they're a pain." Her torn shoes, her overflowing flesh. The wind freezes. She trips. I snuggle up to her. Our hair touch lightly. The wall is light green under the moon. Black water. Rowboats. Venetians, seated, silent, kitchen smells reddened by geraniums. Fat woman. Fat cat. Fountain in the middle of a town square or a courtyard. Fat cat fat woman kitchen smells red . . . your cooking smells of fat woman fat cat courtyard or square of a middle in the fountain fountain in the middle of a square in the middle of a square. We walk aimlessly. We turn around. We back up. We begin again. Compact, stooped body of my mother. I feel alone. I feel lost. Hair that looks burned . . . The columns were waiting for us among my father, the aunt, the cousin, at the end of the alley. "—Oh, sweetie; it's a good thing you have a good husband because with a bitch like that! She can make your life hell. What has she done your poor mother that you sacrifice her? George, he has his job, it's not the same. And besides, he's a man, he can take it. Oh sweetie it breaks my heart to see you bleed yourself white for this ingrate . . . My poor sister . . . I feel sorry . . . You certainly didn't deserve that, you're so kind. Nothing was too good for this child: best schools, private lessons, trips to Florence, tennis lessons . . . For what? So she can spit in your face!" "—Andrée, stop that!" my mother sobs, my father mumbles. The sun is setting behind the windshield. "—Selfish, cries my false aunt, selfish, that's what you are! You're killing your mother." The road grows dark. Venice behind us. The waters of the Grand Canal like black veins. The water. The air. The wind behind, inside. I feel the nylon of her nightgown, soft, the sheets are cool. Her back lightly touches mine. "—Look Ghyslaine, that initial ring, I sure would like to buy it for myself." I drag her away. My mother's arm under my arm. Her black coat against my coat. They bought me. They are not my parents. "—I can say everything. Reveal everything," "—You're crazy," says my mother. The car goes by. My arm detained by a clenched hand. The crowd leans. The traffic is stretched out in metallic and blond strands of hair. A passenger seated across from us stares at my mother. I try to communicate with the seagulls, behind the rectangle of the window, with the wet light. "—Can never have fun with you." My mother like an old sacrificed brat, the price of the menus, her black coat, her opaque belly, her dyed curls. Lulu cries out from the depth of the pink marble and the wrought-iron finials: "—Wow! was it neat! you two old bats. Why did you dump us? We had a ball with old Georgie here. Hey, Uncle Georgie, you showed us a good time, didn't you. And the guard! That guy, I swear! He was worth a laugh. Mamma peed in her pants. Didn't you pee in your pants, mamma. Don't laugh. Admit it. You even poo pooed!" "—Lulu! won't you be quiet, you terrible child." "—Don't move kiddo. You look sensational with a little polka dotted pigeon

there, and the red sky, you look like Theodora, Empress of Byzantium."
My mother, half-flattered, half-melancholy waits, smiles. I shiver."—
Let's go in," "—You don't care, you've been here before. Give me a
chance to enjoy it. Don't spoil this trip for me." The gold. The fleshy
pink. The gate offers resistance: closing time. I don't have much more
time I am told by the black coat, the wig of my mother. As we approach,
something seems to leave the canals, to leave the palace facades, to
leave the silence, to leave the moon, to leave the sun, to leave the
human beings, to leave the Adriatic, to leave the ivy, to leave, to leave,
to leave. We get back on board the boat for the reverse crossing. On the
bridge, my mother's eyes watch the water, the fog, the anecdote,
outlines of the churches, all that she could share with me. Everywhere
mother's eyes, her guts watch eagerly, hoping, but nothing, there is
nothing, only avenues like those we are walking down for nothing. My
mother snuggles up against me. I feel we are miserable, sick as we've
been for many years. "—This dirty water oh no with these bugs it's
rotten I wouldn't live in their moldy rat-infested palaces for all the
money in the world yes and in summer it must be worse when the water
is do you want me to buy you a croissant at this beautiful pastry shop?"
Leaving the snackbar, I burst into tears. My mother begins to cry.

We are home. My mother is hanging the clothes out to dry.

I join her in my room, above my bed, in the white of the wall, then,
at night, as usual, in the empty spaces, in an infant.

What if she did not exist, what if I did not think about her, what if
everything remained mediocre but without my need of her . . . without
my need of her . . . without my lack of her, without my intuition of her
. . . without her ash-blond glimmer, without her skin pale as the milk
I was not given, that must be so soothing to drink, without the flickering
of the blond light, without the ache in my heart, without the desire to
snuggle up inside her belly, to be received in her arms, hidden in her
boundless arms.

I press my cheek against a wall of wool and folds. I see neither torso
nor the face.

Her name and address have been torn up. What did I inherit from her? Is she suffering today? Is she looking for me?

Overpopulated cities of the North where each woman is some part of her. Each year from her belly, from her refusal, like an incision from which I flow. Day before yesterday, war photographs. Northern beaches, velvety like a light touch from her. The too youthful flesh of her back, her shoulders; her music, her lactescence which could not have been vice or inertia.

Each word. Each image, deprived of her maternity.

Authoritarian her proud white neck, her milk, withdraws from where I descend in a blood spurt with nothing from her leaning and she does not look back.

Warm little head, apple flesh . . . I have pressed my cheek against her brand new cheek . . . the baby, she could have held it the way I hold it . . . except it would have been me against her, me against her.

She must have been like the vertical sweep of the Northern houses, like the streets where it rains, all day, near the border . . .

Of her . . . But I came out of her . . .

To expel . . . simply to expel. With all her strength, she pushes. Suddenly out of her comes something warm, hard, wet and screaming.

I was not handed to her. She did not take me in her arms. I was taken away.

The window to jump out of, through her motionless face which does not want me, through my desire for her.

—Selfish! . . . if you gave a little more thought to others, you wouldn't be so unhappy. The past, that's over. What matters is the husband the children you will have.
—She was a monster.

—You don't know . . . you can't judge . . . in wartime, little girl, so many things happen . . . But look for her; make inquiries where I did. Maybe they'll answer you.

—I don't want to know her.

She raises her hand to her chest, to her neck. Her tongue comes out. I should be caressing her wrinkles, the blotches on her face.

—Sweetheart, he whispers to her, without being able to stop anything, sweetheart . . .

Her body quakes with spasms. She tells me, her eyes distorted by the tears:

—Kiss me . . . kiss me.

I push her away. There is no one. The other mother left me in a hospital, one wartime day. She will never come back.

Eyes bloodshot, she shouts:

—If you must blame someone, don't blame us. We are not the ones who abandoned you!

The sky is black. The white lampshade is spotted with countless shadows.

Where to go? What am I looking for? Not this woman who does not exist. To really have her near me. Who? . . . What? . . . An urge to abandon everything, to start over, to leave, the doors lead to open bellies ringed with light, in the sun, to the flesh, to the room. So blonde.

Dry skin. The delicate skins in magazine ads. Millions and millions of women. My nose whose contours are not regular enough to take after her. The blind little center, swollen, almost red in the mirror, above the sink: my mouth. My. Me. The oval. The width of the brow. The hairline. Whose? The beige color dotted with russet. These freckles. Even if the shape of the right eye, small, greenish, is modified, if the left eye . . . It opens wide, it widens, it shifts, it is her eye, it moves in toward the nose, even if the dark chestnut ash-blond hair, fluffy chignon, more beautiful . . . The beige of my murky complexion is an obstacle. Impossible to see her, to go farther. My face becomes hard, thick, opaque matter.

From the Porte d'Orléans to Fresnes: cages, boards, cranes, cables, lines of cars, smoke, bus stops where tired, solitary young women wait.

A walk through Fresnes: puddles of grease from one face to the other, and lime dust.

Fresnes in August: tire blow-out.

Everything is of concrete, of cement: grass, clouds, women's dresses.

A massive highrise that makes human beings down below seem useless.

—If I'm not mistaken you don't like pickles.

Three pylons behind a row of cages. Electric cables above the sky. The ceaseless rumble of planes. Four highrises. Two cylinders under a crane.

All one color: clouds, sheet metal, cement. In the kitchen, through the window, one sees eighty-three cages.

—I've been slaving away for four hours.

Plastered on the sky, seventeen floors of black, seventeen floors of beige, twice seventeen floors of gray. The livingroom: synthetic fur. Polyester varnish, linoleum.

The guard whistles. Rooms opening out onto the balcony between the sheet metal and the cement. Daylight: only between the metal slats of the drawn blinds.

The moment divided into squares and rectangles: rooms. Balcony. Cages. Inflow of dry air.

—What shitty weather!

The warmth pierces the hard matter of the city but the light in the room remains gray, cadaverous. Prefab church crosses. Dusty lawns. Metal of the motorcycles, the television antennae.

The dimestore stuck between two cages. Lacquered corrugated iron. Geraniums planted in reinforced concrete and plastic.

A prefab shanty under the cranes. A second set of cranes. "—Ghyslaine, where are you?" And I could be dead. I could have jumped out the window. Thousands of windows, millions of windows, millions and millions of tenants. Streets like black dug-up roots between lawns and buildings. A bald skull. Diapers hanging.

A trailer in front of the prison wall. Urine. Turds. Spit. Bare turf. In the distance, a dark gray cylinder punctured with black windows.

"—It's funny each time I look up, here, I see new cages." A row extends a row behind a row.

Along the prison wall, my mother walks, head lowered, does the shopping, perspires, carries pounds of food.

Modern crucifixes: three iron cranes above cages.

—Oh! my dress torn, ripped!

A crack occurs at the base of the top part of a ten foot flare releasing gas. The non-desulfurized fuel threatens to increase the percentage of sulfurous anhydride in the air.

Her nose is wide as if swollen by the tears, between the two aged eyes.

She laughs. Her good mood tired and wrinkled. Her gestures abrupt.

—And once again the table has to be set. Eating and cooking and dishes and sleeping, it never ends.

This evening the big city cages shine, cigarette packs.

—Well, I don't understand why they did not find anything on the moon. There must be bugs at least.

—What?

—Oh! well!

—Hey!

—Oh! Well!

—Well, well.

—Good, well.

—M'be I'm going to be to be. I'm splitting because . . . zip!

—Already, sixty-five miles less, Hey!

—You want tweezers for your eyebrows?

—Well, OK I'm eating.

—Oh good.

—Ugh!

—It's not good, but edible enough.

—What!

—Not not good but not first-class.

—What's lousy.

—What?

—These tassles.

Perrier Evian water pretty heart ripe yellow peaches big beautiful tomatoes a package of macaroni.

—Since you are addressing old people a group I am part of this old son of a bitch. How did she manage to find one thousand francs? In that case, you'll have three thousand francs. If I have thirty-three thousand francs, I lose thirty thousand francs. If I have three thousand francs, I then have one hundred four thousand francs. You call that doing social work! One thousand francs. From '66 to '69, thirty thousand francs. In '69, three thousand francs. One thousand seven hundred in '68. I must have seven thousand francs!

—You know little girl, I'm a big guy . . .

—When you've paid the telephone, the car, gas, insurance, the rent, the food, the utilities, what's left?

—He got up again last night, to take a pill.

—Old people.

—A dining hall. Seven francs for lunch, four francs fifty for dinner, and in addition, to sleep in, a cell six feet by eight feet.

—Yeah, Yeah. I don't feel what I wanted to feel. I would have liked to feel more euphoric than I do.

—A new-born, how can that interest a man?. . . This lump of flesh, this limp body, it's not conscious of anything! what makes you think a man cares one way or the other.

. . . Above his soup plate filled with hot crayfish consommé, his lips neatly lined. Between his lips, his thick tongue:

—What's the most unfortunate vegetable?

—I don't know.

—The artichoke: we cut off its head, we eat its heart and cut its hairs.

The belly which secretes the only light.

Brother, sister, for life, still damp from the moisture of her organs . . . The lining is just a few inches from me. Something internal, still beating.

Him:

—When you can't, you can't! No use forcing it. We couldn't: we couldn't! Of course, you always prefer children of your own . . .

The singer taps on the piano and sings: Dites-moi qui a fait les arbres, qui a fait les rivières, tell me who makes the trees, who makes the rivers; her belly, her breasts shake. Tell me who makes the rivers, who makes the trees, who . . .

He whistles under his breath. He looks at me. I look at him.

—Now, on me, water off a duck's back! what I don't want is for you

20

to keep on making your mother suffer.

—My mother?

The 1940 exodus. The line of cars on the roads. The bridge is mined.

—And so, we could have said: we made the gesture, that's enough. But we loved you like our own daughter. I believe we went beyond the call of duty.

In a stroller, a doll, dead baby.

Savages. No pity. Bastards. S.O.B.'s. Colt 45's. Mercenaries. Commandos. Hell. No pity. Hate.

He turns his back on me.

Him:

—You're trying to get me rattled but nothing you can say will bother me, water off a duck's back.

The leg is bare, folded on the sheet. This leg, now adult, having begun to develop without being desired, without being accepted, of live flesh, rejected, anonymous. Low, rounded calf; white, fine skin, thin ankle. No father, no mother; simply expelled.

—Get the hell out of here! I'll never be able to be rid of them. I don't want. Get them out. Out, out!

Read from the bus: savage sex.

"—You don't know, it was wartime, a lot of things happen . . . in wartime, you can't imagine . . . Children in heaps or children who, alone, you don't know who they, where they're . . ." They. The darkness of a living room next to the factories covered with soot, an old woman, her back turned, asks a blond woman: "—So?" From the blond hair, comes a low voice: "—It's done, permanent green of the eyes, I've abandoned her."

. . . Girl or boy . . . she got up, she left. She did not want to see, did not want to know . . . but, saliva and milk bubble in the corner of the tiny lips, the fresh rubber of the powdered thighs, I was of her. Throbbing, swelling days. Eruption. I was her baby.

—No.

—Shit.

—Then.
—Good.
—You put.
—Yea.
—I'm turning out the lights.
—I'm not hungry.

I enter my room at the end of the hall. I lie down. The noise of the children outside, playing, the noise of a plane, the noise of a car starting up, grow, grow in my blood. My heart aches.

Egg embryo fetus child climbs the wall.

—You were a magnificent baby.

—You looked at us as if saying take me, take me.

Clenched in her stiff fingers. Take me.

She: "You have no defects; your spleen was examined." To the folds of their lips, to their protruding eyes, blood-shot, to the mass of their body, my affection handed over like bleeding meat. I was screaming, uncomprehending, obedient, shy, had been delivered to them, maybe born of an artillery shell, of a blood puddle gleaming in the sun but to them daughter of lovers, were shaking me, shaking me, still full of bluebells, of buttercups, of daffodils, of crocus, of snowdrops, of violets, of primrose, of aqueous and warm petals, they crush me.

A counterpane covers the easy chair obstructing the passageway of the bedroom door to that of the balcony. A counterpane covers the tufted headboard of the bed. On the left, between the night stand, the bed, the wall and the French window, a counterpane conceals with its folds and creases, the dressing table chair. Cracks in the plaster draw black bloody vessels. The ceiling crushes. Between the heavy drapes, the dense sky crowds the window. Opposite, the armoire hides the wall almost up to the ceiling. Behind the locked door, the windowless hall. At the end of the hall, the livingroom, extension of the wind, of the cold air, of the skylines of the new subdivisions, of chimneys, of television antennae, of cranes, where, stretched out, barefoot on the hide-a-bed, her torso with large shoulders hidden by the noisy newspaper pages, she reads: infanticide in the basement rape of victim drug death rattle party for hairy naked elderly here is the photography of an electrocuted workman. This man you see above, to the right, will die in a few minutes his head severed.

The walls, the drapes curve in.

Tall, her numerous eyes float. They think about what?

Even with the heads, the shoulders, a swirl of aluminum whistles, shines. The shadows of the airplanes crash brutally; the dirt, the leaves, are crushed.

Porte de Saint-Cloud. Sidewalks in the night without street lights. Demolished walls. Razed surfaces, covered with pebbles. The stroller in which, throat tight, I am seated, rolls on. The inside of a dairy of frozen water. The apron covers a large bosom, large hips. My adoptive mother places a container full of empty milk bottles on the counter. A bottle of cold is handed to her.

Between two slats of the metal blinds, concrete chimneys.

I listen to the cries of a baby, his flesh, his bracelets of fat, to penetrate, the breath of a mother.

We'd put Robert's shoes on you. How old were you? No more than two. You would clown for us for hours. Did you make us laugh! You were very cheerful. I would tell you: The good Lord put you on earth so I could play with you, my little doll. I would put you in your playpen, I'd dance in front of you, I'd act silly, I'd sing, you'd laugh!

The floor covering is slimy. The hall is dilating. They have put Uncle Robert's shoes on me. I am not more than two. I play the clown, for hours. Frail little body of mine, huge black shoes above which I am misshapen, put on earth so I can be played with. And they laugh, seated around my childhood which did not come from a belly but is the doll given along with bouquets of gladiolas, to the woman who underwent surgery, to the woman taking a cure, to the woman who is depressed. The woman puts me in a playpen. Around it, she sings too loud. She dances. She twirls her pleated skirt because her nervous system is out of whack and, supposedly, I laugh, I laugh, I laugh, I laugh, I laugh.

During the meals, look at me their gray lips, their teeth, their nostrils, their hairs.

From the dime store to the highrise: background of smoke. Black and meat-red shopping center.

Holding tightly on to the concrete honeycomb, strangle me and swarm, in the walls and black, pierce, groove, penetrate, flow, clamber, fallen, downed, laugh, laugh, swallow me, crushed, between their teeth without light.

Will meet, will find.

I will never meet her? I will never find her? . . . Our two bloodstreams commingling, her rays, my night. From time to time she turns on the light to feed me . . . her warm arms.

The room smells of urine, of sweat, of pills. Above the sheets, the scattered generating cells, revolve slowly, in the insufferable glow of the lamp.

Women, in a panic, during the bombings, descend, no longer know, leave behind, run.

Her warmth, her nearness shimmer, her cheeks in the sunlight, her lips swollen with seeds. "—If I were you, I'd be ashamed to treat us the way you do!"

I drag myself, drag myself, over the sterile breath, by a need to nurse: "—Here! here's your dough! take it, your dough! Bend over! Crawl. Pick it up, your dough. You have no guts!" Above the ten franc bills that she threw down on the dining room rug, her muscular mass is silhouetted. Did I bend over? No. No. I must not have lowered myself to her screams.

One morning, the straight shore, the water of the North Sea, the dry sand, very blond; the air shines . . .

A few years after the liberation: their chestnut wood sprinkled with cold sunlight, because their fabric shop was prosperous; white, blond arms of a maid, something, in the smell of leaves and earth, yes, something imperceptibly demolished, an automobile too black, with narrow windows, was taking me to discover Paris, to discover the apartment buildings reaching the still haunting airplanes; the sky, beyond the top floors was smoking, so dark . . .

Merry-go-round, afternoon off school, they will not come, street uphill, bright wall, sun, forest behind the wall, they rejected me, where are, did not want to help me and root in the center of a province, my name is empty, my blood is empty, a child is born, it had at first been a sexual desire, in the dust, outside, desire, in the white blouse of a young girl. I close my eyes.

In the hair, in the dark, mine, which I brush in front of the mirror, greenish stain of two eyes, mine, penetrating farther than the war, to the intense green, central, of their original eye where I am lying in the fetal position, but, August 1944, a young feminine body, slender to her flowing hair, rejoicing in the act of surrender signed by the German general, she strolls about, aimlessly, and she blondulates under the plane trees in the afternoon, her stomach flat once more.

Tourcoing: population, 83,400. Big textile center. Lille. Valenciennes. The little dashes to separate France from Belgium. The Northern expressway. The smoke, the rails, the bridges towards the North. Flemish flesh. It could be Lille. It could be Valenciennes, it could be Tourcoing. It would be necessary to know their name. And what kind of factory? Textile is not the only industry in the North. There are a thousand kinds of industries. Thousands.

My mother above her plate containing chicken bones and vinaigrette sauce, says: "—Well, I think that it was her family that was against the marriage." Red bricks. Concrete. Asphalt putty. Fusion of metal in a crucible. Three hundred feet of electric cables rolled up. Acid vats.

A math professor. Maybe he was a garbage collector. She could not keep you. I run. I go down. I rush toward the air, toward the void. I look for her. Her. Her blond hair. The air. The void. Her blond stain. Your mother's parents were. He is lying. I know he is lying. He is lying to me. Little ones. I checked it out. People. Small creatures. Small human beings. There were some in the wheels. The four chrome wheels of the table. No one. They were, you know but . . . Four. A girl of . . . The grayness of his eyes tries to flee toward the rug, toward the wall, to the left.

She was a woman who must have had affairs. He wants to defile her. Father. My father. Your father. Father . . . Your mother; I saw her. She was blonde, tall. She must have had affairs. She was one. I think she was married, she had children, I think. You could have been handed over to some garbage collectors who would have sent you out to beg. We did our duty. She said what she. She was beautiful? You saw her? Was she beautiful? How should I know. I forgot . . . It's been a long time. But you remember, she was blonde, you saw her, she was blonde, you saw her blonde, you told me blonde.

—I don't know anymore. I forgot. Yes. She was tall. You're being a pain.

Father, father. Male. Male of the female. Mother with the wide hips from which flow the fine butter and the fat milk, the blond beer. I go down. Father. My mother so beautiful. You desired her. You lay on top of her because she was blonde, tall, where I begin, where I begin to go down, soft; my mother, in her, I sleep, that the man had chosen, soft; my father who had chosen the woman from whom flows the blond beer, the wine, the fat milk, the butter, on the grateful earth and I was, me, nestled near the beating of her heart.

Certainly she was beautiful, soft, the softest, the finest, so fine, too fine, the rose of wheat, of sensitivity, of frailty, her wide medieval brow chiseled in wood and painted blue and gold, elegant femininity, Our Lady of the Savior, Grateful, aging whore with screaming yellow hair who cackles, who cackles.

—You shouldn't try to find out. It must not have been pretty.

—Why?

—It's never pretty in such cases. You read, he found his mother, and said: never look for her. One imagines her beautiful. His was a drunkard, she had walked the streets, dirty hair.

The day, in my eye, acid drops . . . This limp day of my belly like a porcupine or a crushed bird, internal; moths, bedbugs, pants. You've peed again. It's a defect. Not from us, not from us, but from those strangers questionable like the cleanliness of cafeteria glasses; she changes the sheets, she airs out the room, I would be ashamed of myself if I were you, foamy, bitter, yellowish, full of piss, that she scrubs, that she cannot remove, that she cannot erase from the hard earth. Harder and heavier than the others and woman without ovaries, asleep closed and she took me on her lap. The sky, from her room is like a sticky, whitish liquid. I was sobbing in front of her wide shoulders. I was screaming in front of her wide shoulders. But little girl you were abandoned I cuddle you, I cuddle you, little one, you were a little ball. Smell my breath which gets poisoned by you, little arsenic but little one, I adopt you, I pick you up, I rub you, I pour you some boiling water. There, my little one, there, there settle down. You are mine, mine only, in my kitchen you are mine, no one will take you from me. Go ahead and pee. I will clean up your urine, little sick one, little girl with fragile nerves, you are weak, you would cling to me. Two assholes and don't think about it anymore, they made love.

She was light, her head bent.

The mist of her softness, without being able to prove it . . .

Her satin flesh cheek-bones, her curved brow, the blond electricity of her hair, she, down in my belly like contractions. The child is on its way. I am my mother, full of sweat, pushing, teeth clenched, stopping, breathing in, pushing again, expelling myself. I scream. She does not want me. She abandons me. I call out to her. I sob. She is motionless, flat, far away face, embedded in the plaster of the wall. She contains no one.

Shines gurgles swaddles me but the breasts sweet with drug thighs lips spasms close her gaze her world under anuses lactation crushed resisting of the drapes two darkened eyes ooze down the wall military masses in armor advance determined to keep on advancing m and golden lily on a field of azure door opened onto the sunny countryside oh Our Lady of the Savior answer our prayer angel in stone armor stone head without neck nose chin destroyed one hundred and twenty miles from here buying leeks tomatoes a roast for lunch she meets her children in their clear iris in their blondeness does she feel me Lille an emaciated body a mourning suit cut the way they cut them during the war straight hair motionless greasy sparse dark gray and me hidden a few feet from her or addressing her just to hear her voice the sound of her heart as in the days when we were one outside the clouds the dark green of the trees whistle, draw nearer the mucous membranes of her belly outside the arms the cheeks the necks the legs that nothing anymore can protect and tremble the flesh of milky women soft as kittens as warm birds the uterine cavity for shelter Porte de Saint-Cloud and Boulogne grow sharp grow heavy with the roar a quarter till twelve the ambulances have arrived the blood refusing to come out it wanted to hold back it did not want to stop filling the blood vessels it did not want to stop providing heat to circulate flows out silently onto the street onto the cracked sidewalks a dead dog drips down the bellies of the victims the surviving women men watch fertilized by the soldier who panting raped her the ovum develops I developed month after month maybe the blue of her eyes and maybe the brown of my father's eyes were my closed eyes in the aquarium of her belly my skin of her blondeness and my limbs of her slenderness my tissues were in her imagination and not in her love sad thistle nettle which she did not water which she would never pick her blood nourished me intruder like the rain or the sun I float in the hemorrhage I float in the nearby flesh as if my frightened quivering mother were still carrying me rolling in her unclean hair boobs shrew drunkard harlot who asks for more tart slut teats strumpet tramp bitch fat ass miserable blood my blood the red of the blood the worn shabby woman who has her wrinkles and her rolls of fat licked in exchange for banknotes she stuffs in the inside pocket of her imitation lizard handbag the origin of the blood cells placenta 3,500 water releases her energy throughout the concrete of the city in helmets covering the skulls in shrillness in croaking sunshine in rattles in glistening puddles full of flies of the meat where nothing stops me from rolling out depressed while through a narrow opening I start out head first but instead of reaching the concave blue the luminosity of the water where I yearn to be contained whole naked I descend along the rubble my oppression increases covers me with dust with spider webs with pebbles I cannot stop the descent through the basements through the underground town-halls where pale skinny silhouettes are assembled resignedly waiting and the air is lacking and I walk in the pit of the shadowy underground shelters where no one no car goes by where will never go by will never speak will never breathe will never cuddle on these paving stones connected to the distant houses by severed cords and by expelled organisms breasts dissolved limbs protoplasm of pity under the astral crevices under the branches of dead trees and the gurgling chills the cranes the dredging machines the blocks down always farther down.

DOCUMENT (I)

(I) *On the asphalt and under the bombs of our SICK world, these events have actually taken place.*

—Sir, her parents died during a bombing raid, the one in Boulogne. They were probably on their way to the hospital where the little girl's mother was to give birth. There were three in the car: the father, the mother, the aunt. The car was hit. All three of them died, the father at the wheel, instantly, the mother, given priority, because she was pregnant, the aunt and a group of twenty other victims were taken to the hospital by ambulance. In the ambulance the mother was already giving the death rattle. The child was saved by Caesarean. A few hours later the mother was dead. The aunt died approximately a week later. It is awful, sir. This child, may God bless her, is a miracle. I can assure you, sir, they were decent people, both teachers. The mother was a French professor, the father was a math professor, at the University of Poitiers. They lived in the 18th District. The mother was from the North, her parents in industry, well-off, excellent family, sir, one of those upper-middle-class families. When they brought me the little girl, I knew absolutely nothing about her. I kept the infant, but with reservations, as you can imagine! and I began an investigation. Of the maternal grandparents and the parents. As for the paternal grandparents, also decent people, it is true I did not check. It would have entailed phone calls, and you know because of this zone business, phone calls are difficult. On the other hand for the mother's side, I sent someone up North. I found out the address of the maternal grandparents who had left. They had fled during the 1940 exodus and no one knew where they were. They were elderly people. I must admit I should not have put this child up for adoption, I should have sent her up North, put her in an institution similar to ours while waiting for the grandparents to return. What I did, I admit, was illegal, but no one knew that the grandparents had not been killed and besides they were elderly. Before dying, the aunt

29

said: "—This little girl has no one left to take care of her." It was wartime. We are going to lose her. What counts is saving lives. I was not going to risk her also getting killed out on the road, in some bombing raid. I'm glad, sir, you're the one who took her, you know, sir, she is of good stock, that's what's important, right? What else can I say? The mother was twenty-four. The father was forty. About the mother, our nurse who worked at the hospital and knew her, told me she was a young woman with ash-blond hair, very slender, tall, pretty, very sweet. If I had not known you, if you had not been one of Mr. X's friends... I would not be telling you all this, you know usually, we don't say anything, but I have complete trust in you. This will stay between the two of us.

He answered:

—Since the mother is dead, I don't want to know any more. And in any case, I will not tell the child she is not our daughter. I'm giving her my name so she will never know.

... So you will never know...

It was during one of my mother's nervous breakdowns, since he believes she has a heart attack, that he revealed the truth to me, twenty-five and a half years after my birth...

—If you want to visit their graves, I could get in touch with the director of the institution if she's still alive. She was already in her fifties when I met her. I'm sorry: we always think we're doing the right thing and then we realize we are wrong. If I had known that you were hurting, that that was what was troubling you, I would have told you sooner. But you didn't open up to me.

—But you let me believe... You not only kept quiet but you lied to me.

—I wanted to hide the truth from you; it was so sad, and then you hated violence so much... Your mother didn't know anything. I didn't want to tell her. If your mother had known, she would have lived in the fear that the grand-parents would claim you one day. No. They must not have known anything. They were probably told: your daughter was killed with the child she was carrying. It's your mother who went and told you that we had adopted you. I'll never forgive her. Your mother told you all she knew. She believed that you had been abandoned since 90% of the cases at that institution were abandoned children. I didn't contradict her. I thought it would be best for you not to learn the exact cause of your adoption that is the bombing raid, the tragic accident in which your father died instantly, in which your aunt and your mother were mortally wounded and in which, from your dying mother, you were born. When we chose you, your mother was with me. They told her, I remember, that your father was a professor at the University of Poitiers and that your mother, daughter of Northern industrialists, taught French. The woman asked your mother: "—Do you want to know anything else?" Your mother, moved to tears, answered: "—No." A week later I returned to the place, and that's when I got all the information. If I had insisted, I could have found out the name you should have had . . . !

—Why did you try to make me think they were lowdown? You distorted them for me? You respected neither the truth nor their death?

—So you would not regret them. So only we would exist for you.

They are dead. Killed. Dead. She is dead. Worn, pieced together, the oval of her face leans over a long, dead body. Her light hair. Oh! her light eyes! nowhere!

On the waters, toward the sun, moves the pink smile of her breasts, of her swollen belly but it is no longer she, she is black, covered with scales, she stands straight, facing forward, rigid, without a sign of life, carries me in the cold bones of her arms while she lies there, stretched out while her womb throbs, while I am being born like the last drops of her flesh, of her warm marrow.

Draped in flesh, veins full of blood, the lady wrapped in sunshine, the sparkling, creamy and salty lady to be suckled, show your belly! I am like arms at the ends of your arms and my heart is snug, so tiny, in your radiant heart. You possess blood and milk. Before you appeared, before the rays so near, so intimate of your shape, everything was floundering, was false, before you appeared, draped in flesh, veins full of blood, everything was floundering, was false.

War death prostitute blood rape abandonment fear unknown destruction and tenderness sky of flesh knowledge are united in you to the rhythm of my need of you and of my pain at having been abandoned by you are blended in you are unfurled over my life in the silt in the shimmering.

31

You who are made of water like the sun, like the clusters of stars warmly shining on your hips, the light dallies in your blond tresses, coiled up like fern, your glorious flesh, spangled with the shadows of leaves and buds your skin diaphanous like stained glass the flesh of your cheeks too white as though they might be made of tiny icicles, oh! if you could sprinkle me with your water! oh! if you could sprinkle me with your water! image of moist flesh, overgrown with moss and lichen, where the light gently filters! Identity, vulva mangled with fits and shell-holes, mights of crevices, of bacteria, of mildew. She is with some guy who is not your father. Black hospital of a bombed avenue. Blonde.

From reality to me there were, so close, already and so sought after, your flesh, your hair. In delirious pain, I learned to know you, to feel you.

And you are not that.

You are dead. Frail. Private. Maize skin, mangled muscles.

The books that she preferred, that she studied, that she discussed with my father, who will take them? They are sorted out on the shelves of the library, literature, philosophy, science, her books against my father's books, her cheek, her vaporous ringlets, often, leisurely, as she dreamed against my father's cheek and they cover, dusty, yellowing, coming unglued, the seams splitting, the wall of the little room in the apartment no one airs out, no one unlocks. She is carried away, lying on a stretcher. Her hair hangs loose. The clear morning sky breaks away from her, begins to darken. She is giving the death rattle. The blood erases her face. Under the gathers of her beltless, water dress, her belly is white, smooth, oblong, convex, a large egg.

Toward your frail body, they are rolling, watch out! they are rolling over you, watch out! over your frail body, flesh which spills out like dark fallen petals, bloodred moss of your crushed flesh on the ground, your dead matter scooped up now, with a shovel and you cannot grow.
Of the woman, there is nothing left. Only, at times, in the clouds or in the water, a human eye. Of the mother, there is nothing left. Only a sexual triangle which at times lights up in the clouds, like a dove.

The red of a setting sun through black branches, the red ochre of deserts, the red of a wound, streams from her throat, from her breath into the flames. Ahead of me the earth extends to its invisible curve.

And now I have only to walk, to continue to walk, there, where you could not continue, on the ground, in the air, under the sky transmitted by you while above me, as though you were dilating toward them, all the suns of worlds perhaps not yet alive, flicker in the gases and the dust of black space.

All that you penetrate, you make fertile, oh mother. All that you penetrate, eventually ends up shrinking its degenerate matter and dies like the stars, oh mother, so that buds will reappear, childhood will reappear, and so you, shining more and more brightly above agony, murder, injustice, pain, you become more intense, alternately creating and destroying, cherishing and abandoning, with equal strength to total purity when, at the end of the world, the sun will have inhaled the earth, the planets will have mingled, the galaxies will have merged, the universe will have become once more a big fiery belly for the new explosion of flowers and seeds, in spite of despair and death, that which her blond hair, invisible, had that was so good, so soft, toward new worlds, in the new language where maybe there will be no more casing, no more shape, no more colors, no more lines, no more isolated and abandoned flesh, and maybe no more destruction, no more sacrifice, what, in spite of despair and death, had that was so good, so soft, her blond, invisible hair.

But you are not that.

In a subterranean odor of dead organs, constant gushes of concrete and cement, build the obstruction, street where I search while beneath, blood seeps from the cracked soil, slaughter instead of the gardens which I do not dare look at because to life we must become adjusted. The black wind batters the solitary screams, twirls soiled papers, sanitary napkins, poisoned rats, expels from its anus, the panting, devouring embraces against the walls. Emaciated bark at the crossroads protected by sand bags and radars the hysterics. The barricades, the electrified barbed wires close off the air from the sea, the slain processions crumble. Morbid temptation then to stay on the hard bare ground, pressed, false, in the false pretense of your punctured, chafed arms where can be contained all refusal. That which I sleep and which squeezes winds I am sinking my vertigo rolls crushes me, doctor crushes me listen to me and the cast of the round stone brow under the caress but I caress only but these stone eyes of a sadness which has never lived chiseled sentiment nailed to the wall instead of a virgin right on my chest nullified mother nailed by all that is shock strikes machine-gun movement martyrs emerging from the pregnant flesh young dead lying face down under the torrential blood in the wreckage of the planes of the toppled cities armed copulation, mass to be crumpled, over coals, the air dynamites and smashes and soft, white, soft, all of them white, as though they were not stiff, as though they were not lifeless, the legs, the arms of the small corpse hang from the large hands of the father and the small round skull tilted back is stained with the black holes of the wounds. The cranes spin above the apartment buildings where births are encircled with continuous bursts of fire, above arrests, attacks and tortures, above victims of similar blood while the milk of nursemaids spurts out.

Mother, sometimes as though you could not manage to exist . . .
I hurt, alone, very weak, born and walk doubting this kiss mingled with destruction and I shiver, stumble alone.

Near the cannons, near the mined, desiccated cradles, however, my mother lives, her orange dawn, her silk lace, her rain, in me and around me. Even where the vomits, the diarrheas, the rumbling and warm blood are thrown up, my mother at times calms me, embraces me, a smile envelops me like very fair arms and she holds me tight.

Above, light up, below, light up, above, light up, below, light up, yellow lines, gray lines, yellow lines, gray lines, light up, multiply, stack up, streak, furrow, tight, between which no air can pass, repeat triangles, without respite, triangles on the thick blue coating, on the slush concealing walls, ceiling, library, doors, closets while go up, go down, go up, left, lower, the straight lines of the shelves, go down, curl, go up again, go down again, the rest submerged under the blue which flickers with triangles. They are miniscule, they stir, they obsess this thick blue mud which thickens, hallucinates.

Night, no sounds of sobbing. Eyes wide open, to learn, no sobbing.

On the eye in the process of overflowing its limits, under the tumbling of clusters, on the patches of afternoons polishing the bark and through the sweater stitches and the shadow dissolves, the antennae, the stalks, the mustaches, the stones, the ants, the flies, the seaweeds, the milt, the twigs spread out. The sun provides roundness to the fusing decomposition, the bust tiny at the center of the tall bust, near the cradles near the pulpy insides, each baby by each mother is given air, sun, each mother, her baby, her babies, each baby, its mother with countless arms, with countless breasts in the angora enclosure. Palms of lifelines, moistness still more grainy, still more mammiform than before, you emerge, glisten, expand, others. But metal casing and to grow shatters but you darken but from below, growls pulls to contradict decomposes to knock down exudes slaughters damages uproots crumbles shocks castrates no longer to move and the ribbed continents cast anchor clatter explode take aim at each other touch each other to rot the wombs and persecute covered with hair and tongues in the salty bumpsy-turvy gullies smokes croaks yells bleeds whistles and also the epidemics and the end, the inhuman night as long as will not be met, not be known, not be penetrated, not be understood, not be felt, not be present, not be defined, not be identified, not be produced, not possible.

The groves, the grainy trees, the sandy hillocks stretch far away, below, but the blond hair, a glimmer, with its bosom whose curves quiver and recede and from which air and wind emanate, through the interior warmth and the oily canal, slowly it lets the child of fertility descend and bestows upon the day the small living body so the little plump bare feet will no longer dangle in the void, in the darkness, and so that the brown branches, the oil, the diurnal soil of home, he will touch them, he will live in them, he will be absorbed by them like food, like the physical sweetness of an ample cheek penetrating us and so he will break out in sunshine in the heart of us.

Piers sunny with plants; reflection of underwater gold dust where, between the nearby branches and among the sea urchins, behind the insects and the speckles, so many sky-lights ruffle, sparkle in a circle, on the edge of the waves of sparks and the mossy surface of the room and the tulle of the cradle and the fresh paint. Barely swaying to and fro, the baby clothes flap, float, never stopping, above the heart, above the belly, vaporizing in warm twangs, through the mouth. Sunny central canals curve, mingle, spring out of the greenhouse so feathery, so bulging with eiderdowns, amid the movement of the red cabbages, the water lilies, the sweetbriars dangling in the water, in the sodium, in the hormones, in the fats, in the calcium, in the potassium, in the globulins, in the sugar.

And renewal? you? all of you? all of life? now that, in the piped destruction, and in the split person, and in the pain and in the refusal and in the confusion, you yourself begat yourself, now grow, now that you have to begin like this little child born in and suckled by what is good in you, by what is soil, sweet, in you, by what you cannot make use of, by what is work, pursuit of research and knowledge, growth and love, relieves you of your illnesses and of your wear and tear, finds once again the day's strengths.

Beyond your own mother and your own life.

Blows.

And leaps.

II. *Portrait*

Let's tackle this differently but for this quest for a refuge, does there exist a support, an appeasement different from the spiritual molecules of imaginariness, different from the words and sentences which fail to flee from us? Naturally sweet, it will organize itself, it will brighten, it will acquire precision, it will personalize itself, it will communicate, it will unite us, it, portrait broken up of what man has forever been taking away from man, now we must be reborn, we must have it together, it, warm, our well-being, our life, but we are not aware of that fact, innocence but we do not return to it, we are dispossessed of our truth, we do not recognize you, when, among our warts papulous with intolerance, we crush your true face, oh! my child's sweetness!

Under. a bombing raid. dead. was killed. victim. taken to the hospital in an ambulance. gave the death rattle.

The little flowers of a printed cloth burn, nestle me in gold dust, in their scent, in their ashes, the borders become frayed, I ascend the mothy, spotted gleam, the pockets droop, the stitches, everywhere I penetrate, get loose; the material cracks, moulds itself on the loss of tracks on an imprecise body, on the impossibility, on the shadow. But I try to back up.

Cellar, contractions, flexions, folds, sinuosities, intestines, of her belly and of her whisperings. Mildewed sacs cover the partitions. And crushed, elastic, vatted, she rests, she bubbles up, she ferments, she turns into alcohol, into glycerin, into nappy protuberances; her reserves of sweetness bristle with papillae like an intra-uterine tongue licking.

Her blouse, the milk boils, swaddles, kindles and the egg of the day is served, digestible, with salt and sweet butter for the sippets. In the silver of the mirrors where gold is applied leaf by leaf, in the prism light whose glass panes reach the ground, the solar specter is formed, reformed. The smiles (the mother and her child, one in the other, in the center of the nursery rhyme) gleam. The rays of the organdy are reflected on the surface of the clouds and the atmosphere, continuously stirred by the blond currents, absorbs the warmth of the flesh. The room is wrapped in a gauze of mist, of drizzle, mizzle produced by the breathing of the mother dandling.

Virginity exudes. The rush of blood impels him upright, hard. Facing noon, facing the swelling and the reddening of the clusters, he sniffs her, nibbles her, crushes the sway of her torso, squeezes its pulp, she grumbles. The taut membrane at the entrance of the girdle is ripped. The friction penetrates the skin, the lubrication and sets its velvet on fire, in motion and the ripening secretes the hormone. Inguinal loam between tendrils. In lively effervescence, the nostrils, the navel, by the pollen and by the oils, are led toward the wine bouquet. Beyond the offal region. Beyond the confined domestication where the family, where the necklines lock themselves up in inverted dyads. And she drinks in the air and her bosom swells, voluminous and palpated masses, excess weight of fat, slopes which springs and arteries perceptible to the touch of hands and lips irrigate, without drying up.

The August maturescence unravels the strings, parts the straps, wrinkles her lingerie. She jabbers, she preens, then, pilose, pottering, plump vulva, springs from the bouquet. And from now on, her limbs, her foliation as it embraces, bears fruit, throat like a tree of life ceaselessly renewing youth, food, knowledge. Then the man, as though he, the sky, the parsley, the sun, the seeds, the ladders, she would encircle them all together, merges with her rolls of fat, with her adipose loam, from which rise the gas, the particles, the thermal rays, the sea water drops, the spores, the bacteria, the fumes. And the chest projects, the nipples where excreting canals flow perforate the layers of muslin. The folds, the darnings, the scallop, the hem, the Valenciennes lace of her camisole, bind her, bulge, balloons of bulbous lettuce, corn salads with full hearts and ample seeds, ripe cabbages, melon balls, pumpkins weather-beaten by the sprinkling of drizzle and the air. The flesh puckers under the caresses and the wind. He loves her the way a newborn takes shelter in the opulence where the mound of stout mamma quivers. The smile encircling the blond ripples of the brow propel the blood; the radiance beats through the iridescence, through the mirrors, through the glass bells, through the window-frames, through the veil. The man, under the shower of sunshine, looks at this face set aglow by the skin. Outside the whaleboned lace brassiere, the freshly bathed breasts welcome the saliva, allow themselves to be squeezed, bunched by the fingers, by the nails trying to penetrate their creamy, their mellow, to knead, to fashion flesh rooted in the hoed and ploughed loam. And the mounds of fat collapse, perspire, irritated, inflamed moans where foam the cellulite, the pilosity, milk, champagne of these lumps covered with snails, with grasshoppers, with ants and with hickeys. The gums pull away from its cluster the nipple gaping, flaring. The cellular tissue relaxes, allows the juice to flow, the bubbles to surface, the glug-glug. The man gets out of breath from sucking her. He clutches her, her carnation, her plumpness, her armpits padded with fat and with vessels, and with lymph glands and with nerves. He struggles against the weaning when he will no longer digest, when he will no longer burp, when his stomach will be wrenched from the gastric palpation of the two smooth-skinned globes which he is swilling. Blond hair scattered in space by the air, fastens on the sun, on the beak, on the feathers. Under his hands, the breasts remain wrought like a master-piece. And he sips in small gulps, and with his lips the cutaneous breathing of the bust which, under him, shivers in the meadow whose clover, alfalfa, heather, lavender, goldenrod, lungwort, coleseed, throw a vegetable light on the naked parts of the body, on the frothy gauze, on the dimples set in a scalloped edging, on the silver thread, on the ribbons. He bites the skin in which the gland is wrapped. The pigment, created by the stroking and the rubbing, absorbs the rays. The man becomes excited as though he were trampling grapes for preserves; as though he were wriggling out of it the certainty of never losing her. And he drinks straight from the churn, while, having sat up to fix her hair, she tries to cram her doughy breasts into her tight fitting blouse whose darts are coming unsewn.

This blond halo set deep in the concrete of the wall or in the skull, false escape window under which I call out, still not recovering, under which the headache rises and the vein in my arm, swirling and without stages, will reach only hemorrhage, only the slash in my wrist, only the steady flow of my blood, of the bad weather . . . and to scream, so that, exact point where the fusion takes place from which are derived eggs, cells, you give birth, your aroma, your buttered taste.

The vibrations and the waves of the liquid underbrush. It smelled good of fish at the downy center of the salt and of a breathy mist embossed with young shoots. It is raining on the seaweeds, in the middle of the road-shedding rays of sky, shining, fullness of apricot, in front of the sprinkled edging and the woman facing into the wind, resins right in the hay and the placenta of the meadows, right in the chirping of the elytrons, right in the sandy bottoms of ovaries, is still seated on the ground ready to give birth; she bathes, in the heart of the trees, her breasts like milk seaweeds, among the strawberries and permeates.

But torn from her own legs, her own neck, her own arms which, now, in blood-red nests, in shreds, encircle her like the snuggle of her lifeless flesh.

The townhall, the open-air market, the hotels, the gabled houses, a souvenir shop, the cathedral, their facades carved with finials and roped mouldings, embroidered membranes, filigreed with cornices, with rosewindows, with pointed arches, with redundant ledges, with portals and with corbellings, outline the street hollows where the outside noises arrive like gurgling sounds wrapped in cotton wool, thus you rest in the east, in the south, in the west, in the north, fat, attired in starched organdy, in lace ruches and you quilt with your skin whose paving stones in front of the death wheels, emit a snowy, creamy dough, under the ribbons, rise up in globules, in fleshy scales, in milk foam, in turgescent little cushions, substance fingered with veins against which there is weeping from a desire to lean the endless cheek.

The blood, after having come across the layers of muscles, seeps from the roof of the muzzle. The floor of the tongue, between the canines and the hunting fangs, is struck by the drops which, in sheets constantly renewed, spread out, dark red, on abdomens and crushed apartment buildings. Free, its clouded underground fur with the dense texture of war victims where an orphan tries to find out the identity of a hemorrhage, to see a stature and a face, the carnivore is silhouetted against the night.

The windows move forward, pull away from the surface of the still membranous wall and from the white marls, from the sands, under the chips, behind the ropes, behind the convulsed pipes, now cut. The child walks backwards, the peaks, made of dull grass, shoot up. The child, quivering and gelatinous ball, contracts. The night, hard, stiff, casts its claws, its jaw flaps, its leaps. The child, backed up against the kitchen concrete, compresses his stomach, attempts to increase the space between him and the globs of black saliva which, under the soles of the caterpillar vehicle, ripple toward the child, encircle him with whips of halo growing dim, crawl, lashes, long hazy streets, become entangled, under the cold suctions, collide with one another, multiply, gaseous, like a center hit by darkness dilating, spreading in squadron flying over, continuously, the clover, the grass, around the broken windows of the abandoned nurseries, the flower-beds straight as bones and flattened, razed ground where the mouth of the cannon, in order to reach, shifted in accord with the desperate movement of the live circles outlined by what was still running having been evicted from its home, what clung to the will to flee, to continue developing, held on to the luxurious lace partitions while, from afar, and from above, the piercing, blushing with blood function was taking aim.

Blocks. Rocks. Butts which cartridge pouches, the wrought iron, the slings reinforce, these masters are planted, vertically, in pieces of human bodies, in crushing of bubbles, of lips, of lobes and behind a visor of smoke, they lie in wait, scabrous, they scrape, so that on the loose ground, only hillocks of refuse could be crossed by the currents of sperm and of full moon, by the flashes of wings, by the snug and warm fetuses, in the amniotic fluid, by the breathings, by the larvae which, in numberless melees crawling, rippling, flock to the entanglements of assault, of impact, of schlague.

With blood-red sparklings, muscle, in torrents, swollen, burrower into the most intense in her so moist, so visceral, so arched and their wrapping in the warmth of the pit, emits ovoid organisms which the porous muff absorbs from the loam from which, maybe, after having forded the darkness of the burial, the wailings will emerge dense.

(Will she succeed in stirring you? Not a single limit, not a single type define her, not even the restriction of belonging exclusively to one species. She must, relentlessly, avoid giving you the illusion that she is an individual but grow and, then, breed, transfigure you, by populating you, having propagated.)

She loses her human shape, she burns, marrow of the explosion, she rattles, splintered, sensitive elasticity of the shell-struck space, a whirl of necklaces and bracelets, in the hollow of the layers of the viscera, the morning attached to her lively hair, she bleeds, in straight lines, in streams, in rays, in filaments, in furrows.

Above the cushions, in the middle of the hollow still warm inside, the satin-stitched ruffles overlap the window, flush with the carpet, in the bedroom of polished, carved wood, at the heart of the mud and the soil, which, through the window, connect with the sluices, the galleries of fog, behind the rhubarb. The adhesion pushes the tubes, and the filaments come loose from the muslin, coil, branch out, extend their boughs, the waverings stretch out through emigration, arms joined together whose neckpiece takes shape and contracts, white, the distant sky scatters them, the child resting against the cushions, continues, however, to wait; he imagines the fusion, the coming of the presence, its spongy sheaves.

The scraps of presence, after having been a glance continually holding out microscopic arms toward each solitude and pulling them back, are this large mollusk with stupefied eyes spread out over the dryness of the surfaces, outside of all communication but just where, absurdly, excessively, is still clinging our need to be near. The gestures, the voices, multiplied in a collective tumor of escape imagined like an orgy of clouds of thin gas and cosmic dust, torture each other, fragments of couples and groups and worlds, with the energy released by our disintegrated calls and toward the central zones of an antistellar night, slide, while it turns slower, while the luminosities weaken, while the masses shrink, while the temperature falls, in a retrograde movement of our whole trust.

Among the security lights and the police dogs, a girl jumped from the wagon. The farms, the placenta, the provinces, are decomposing and the spikes scrape and to go to whom?

The translucent brick of the shining buttresses. The battered facades with overhangs, jutting out from the sarcophagi of their ground floors and curved, stars, fruits, domes, globes, teats blurred they are so close, lead out to the water womb, to the intimate bonding under us, thus rises the city without distances, the fat cheek, the fleeting architecture of the carnal touch which we skirt floating on the membranes, the dilation of the structures. Amid the black of death, a full moon of fertility tries to recompose, vibrant, sound casing, a puff, a breath, a roulade, a trill rising from the liquidian environment, something human, feminine, sings, mausoleums, hymns with cupolas, high stories above windows with tabernacles, vast galleries over the sea, chalk of the curdled milk, continuous melody which lost, so young, the reality of her arms, of the soft strength of her arms, the moistness of her warm lips so near the arms, the swelling of her breasts, and her language sings once more.

He stays I want to open the doors the walls the child shakes the door door to what door from where only the unhealthy constructions which are inhabited by the last human pulsations.

Melting away of cosy caves, of tubes, of mountains, the hercynian castration, this ligneous region, under the ocular tentacles trying to see, under the tactile tentacles trying to touch, under the aimless attempts; I smell, the abandoned motors pollute, still smoke, the ground, chassis, crooks, crusts, to stretch to the horizon, its armor-plate, its scrap iron, ransacking me, twisting me, raping me with squalls of absence.

Here is the moss, the tops of the chestnut trees, of the pines, of the oaks, of the hazelnut trees, a stretch of life, matter, heart of the wood, polished, frameworks, hutch, timber, childhood wood floors, drinking in the rain, the dew, the fog and her body, mother and daughter reciprocally, meanders, shimmers, between the shores, she is lying down, grassy, airy, brook; her cheek, the batiste sheets, to kiss her, shine like sweetbriars and morning glories, her down protected me from the cold, I draw from the coal the sap, the vapor as the light hits the boughs when she puts her hands on my fear: "—You have a bobo another have bobo have bobo here?"

Black from the soil whose mulch has been drained, machines, country, wide place, the ground takes back: lost contact, roads of deprivation, forests set on fire, even if we cry out for the flesh, the animal and vegetable soil to return, even if we examine the pale jelly on the move, the inside of the translucence continuously changing shape, cytoplasm of despondency around the kernel of mourning where the shadow woman in the background holding tightly against her, outlines of a child, the emaciated spasm which she rocks with the sounds of her slopes. And the ravaged ground continues, like the space of the rattle where the air passes now only through barriers of mucus.

Under the peaks of mud among the ducks, the bread is set beside the cupboard, behind a bus stopped in front of the bakery. Curtains of a bedroom opening onto a pond, the swelling of the future mother are embroidered in the wind, by the organdy, by the first fruits, by the lace, by the knotted ribbon, and one enters slowly in the *terra cotta* half-light in the blue and orange of four-leafed clovers, of buttercups and roosters hand-painted on the stoneware, in the aviary, in the hot water bottle, in the basket of her belly amid the reeds and, relieved of the wear and destruction, one moves toward the seed of the earth, through the water hairy with tentacles, tubes, eyelashes, gills, cords, barbels, spikes, placental vessels, mouths, floaters, straps, prickles, fins. In the center, the hut adheres to the leaves, is hemmed in, the glass, the larvae, dissolve, frog's-bits with floating leaves swell up and open up, soaked shells ripple, lose their outlines, tongues snatch, coil up, fade out, the alluvium sprouts on the parts of the fence where tentacles break through the greenish water, a magma of frogs, of water lilies, of branches, of ducks, of hydrae boils, the bloodstream is eternal, the filaments of the hut uncoil, sprawl out, shade the contact, the shrubs under the nurturing water and hold you very tightly, spreading out a cover of arteries, of uterine veins and of low clouds, wrap you in a storm, right in the forest seeds, the mud.

Always, always closer to her, without ever succeeding in touching her, in feeling the beat of her pulse, still blond, even the part of the nape of her neck.

Someone silhouetted against the silence, across from the pool of fuel oil, across from the canker, leans against the parapet of the seaside resort subway.

"—What are you doing here? he tells the child. It will be twilight soon, the light is getting dim on the surface of the oily liquid. You must hurry."

The child:

"—Can't you feel that my heart is bursting with fear? You are looking, fisherman, on the other side of the parapet, at the uninhabited surfaces from which nothing comes to your stall, at the reflections going out, at some turtle doves of oxygen, slowly, again shaking free of the wounds. More and more is swallowed, between the pilings, rising, to the banisters, rising some more."

And to the aerial feet of skin whose reproductive umbrella has been torn out, the child hangs, in the hairy membranes.

On the surface the blood gushed in spurts, and on the surface of the hair, the roadway of the boulevard was fluted into the muslin adorning the flesh; the lace because of the pieces of sheet-metal still caught onto the woven gold threads and onto the openstitches, bristles, around the convulsions.

The sheet-metal elements, the automobile, the location now in pieces where, then, was she? where, to the hand of the driver did she cling, unable to flee? shrapnel slices through the heart muscle through the car window and through the skin; advance toward sheet-metal elements as though they were trying to put her chest back together, the creamy chiaroscuro of her arms at the instant she was snatched by the explosion, assemble, slide, speed up, spread out, chassis, on the jumbled surfaces, clutch, waste away, words expelled from her remoteness, like a screen of lank bones, their liquid, translucent silk, barely out of my need of her, hardens in the poisoned air, produces this hardness of the black sheet-metal and of the splayed skeleton . . .

What strokes could refer to her life, restore her forms stirred by the wind? resolve her absence? reach her entrails? the dead woman, the high tide of the dead woman, the decomposed caress, the debris of the room where the little girl while seeking her mother's heartbeat crawls in all directions? and the woman is dead wherever I may go.

The little girl feels her feet sinking into the muddy blocks of butter, into the cheese of snow, into the pails of boggy milk from the inner courtyard. A drape, a cardinal-red night gown, stagnates, like human blood in a hospital basin. The draping, above the charred branches, molds the emaciated, deserted shapes, that block the flow of daylight and air. The wrought iron balcony is worn on the bare curdled skin, on the bare motionless pale of the rows of land-slip compressing.

Burnt grass and hay, disheveled hair, hemorrhages, sway, smoke, lie strewn about the paleness at the level of the honeycombed stonework, hang.

A few miles from the estuary, the little girl leans over a bridge railing, she looks, unable to tear herself away, at the empty shells, at the fringes of limestone, at the needles made of crystal, at the strands made of sand, at the debris covered with scales, at the lace made of salt, at the globular gravel, at the green pigment of the mud, sad alluviums.

Above the oars of her ribbed legs, the sensory areas of her skin, of her glands absorb the stitches of her blouse, she breathes, leaning against the stuffed back of the sky and the leaves, she skirts the fog with which she swaddles the child.

In the steam of the wash house dazzling with sheets, with compresses and with bandages being washed, the little girl touches, caresses, the congealed blood—spit? vomit?—on the marble of the dilapidated dressing table among the globular spiders spangling.

In the bare steel and aluminum, the little girl changes shape, twists, ripples, stamps the ground, squirms but, from time to time, the particles of her fuzzy reflections, through the tears, stop swirling, come near her, come together, let out, in the state of lambency, almost a human breath.

The hair turns grayish, becomes covered with dust.

The little girl snuggles up under the gauze of a mosquito netting, looks at the appendages of the waves, under the salt-encrusted window panes. The casino is gutted. The chalky prickles move, the arms get tangled up once more, the shaggy mouths open up, balance themselves on their shadow lined with curling straps between the rags and the webs.

Hollows of the collarbone, veranda of a belly and of full breasts, glassworks, ventricles of the funeral kitchen on the pieces of glass where the droplets swell.

In a nook, the edge from which come the warm air, the down, the feathers, the cotton, the filaments, the little curls of breath which, in the fatty rolls of flesh, in the folds of the dough, foam, it is raining.

The veiny neck takes on a graceful contour, egg from the earth, egg from a hen throbbing, clucking and of straw, deep in the reeds and the saliva where the combs, the swelling steam, suspended in the atmosphere, brood.

In the sunshine, she was having lunch, the plump downy, still somewhat cartilaginous daisies on the little feet, the little hands, in the dimness of gurglings, in the liquid bulk of herself, tickled her.

The empty shirt is unfolded, spread out, its creamy layer rises, swells in small balloons, cradle, butter rustling, muslin so frothy now sailing, carrying the child, soothing her, sprinkling in her need to suck and the child's fingers feel her, rumple her, squeeze her, she squirts, time for a few gulps.

Between the banisters and through gaps, the child spies upon the decay of the quarters, the samples of human blood on index cards, the public records files.

Chubby-cheeked from the mountains exhaled by the water towers, the cattle-bells, the cow-bells, through the red corpuscles filled with forests under the clouds.

Village with good streets softening the sun, the moon, the sky among the screens, the consoles and the pedestal tables, in the intimate, in the truth of her, of her sinew, of her tissues, of her bones, of her humors and of her viscera.

Disgorge, stagnate, descend, mine, spread out, bile, bubbles, blockhouse, artillery, führer of slobber on the inflamed skin, on the itchings.

In the eddies of screams, in the alcohol soot, rancid, which must be pushed, where the child does not see, where her fingernails scratch and pierce her muscles which during the crises, are hardened by the effort, where the concrete of the road is felt, where the oxygen no longer reaches, where her young child's arms crack and swarm, overripe, filth, at the foot of the wall meat beginning to climb.

It is a cardiac room without breath, without food, where the bruises, under the face powder, under the blond veil of little curls and of eyelashes, after the explosion, light up the inside of the dimples, the inside of the eyelids like a pilot light in the center of the blood on the sheets.

The chest, the buttocks, the ears so warm fashion the nest of the smile, she has sloping shoulders, she creams, spurting of the gymnasium and the red light of the blood vessels irrigates even her clay.

Beyond the hedgerows, the nets, the silks, a bloody mist seeps through the interstices of the blinds and the little girl passes through baskets of fish, furniture of cockles and shells, the membranous phosphorescence of the oysters while the arms milky with salt keep pressing her against the foam, against the frothing.

The mud of the woods glows with hyacinths, speckles the water in the ruts, the furs; the little girl, through the embroidered openstitches of the caul, watches the seeds grow, throw a buttery light, whose veil, splashed with sunshine, swells.

How to get there? Exhaustion gets worse. To be afraid. The nearer the little girl comes to this brightness whose starless night is burned by the wind, this window, this billowing silk and egg yolk on the lunar loggia, this porthole whose flesh she often almost touches, the regular beats behind the gratings, more flaccid, more chitinous on the legs, mass where slobber rats, whips gum up, flay, flog, trickle from the rattle the more frequent are the outbursts, the beast, shaking her, laying her out on the ground unconscious.

The oily mud of the blood rolls, carts, uproots, descends, agitates, erodes, spreads out, on the sides, on the belly, on the scarf, on the woman's coat. The tatters of magma mass up. I see a funeral urn, the irreversible, the light darkened by a clot, small heavy sac, it is I blood-red, huddled, falling. The womb is panic-stricken, gaping, above the void. Fingers, hands are not there to hold me, to keep me, to prevent.

Farther on, above, the ivory of the flesh shines under an embroidered bodice, but the access routes to the teats, to the nipples, are steep streets metallized by the agonizing moonlight and tinted blue by the membranes, the veins and the fins caught in the unknown and in the ice.

(Or else would she be alive if we had not been so weakened? If with enough energy still flowing forth, we would work at reducing to zero our sufferings, our murders, our illnesses, our attrition but what is most heartrending in our desires, in her absence, does not dash toward, does not evolve toward the effort to grow, to become free.)

The waves of the hair suffuse the polychromy with a golden background.

Smelling bad, the little girl walks through the rings in the process of degeneration that the bony tiles, the plaster debris, the cotton wool of the stopper, frost up, do not block up, and she emerges in the open air where the icy silence, the cement of the ice-barrier, the oozings, glassy town, throw phlegms of anemic light.

At the parochial crossroads of the bosom and the arms, the breathing flushes the host, protects its warmth, dandles in the wet gold of the swaddling clothes, of the sheets, of the pillow, of the christening gown and of the diaper, this is where tenderness, relic and transmitted through the sensitive tips of the skin, burns like a taper between the ovoli of the gallery and the liturgical embroidery of the support bows.

Mortuary chapel.

A province laid to waste, its vigor crushed in the weathering, in the cinnabar of these maternal cheeks, shell-struck, muscular acres, whose climate weaves, disheveled, through the fingers of the praying child.

The little girl makes her way across a plain of spindles, of fibers, of fibrillae, of striped marshes, of biceps, of triceps, the hemoglobin, the meadows of bellies and of tendons, the pectoral slopes, the fear, the smooth vastness of the edges of the roads, of the torn layouts, this slaughter giving off, below the horizon, the hemorrhaging rays re-flected, diffused by moans.

The boards shake among the stumps.

She has put on field peas and alfalfa, a dress of ritual lamps, a garb of shrubs and variegated hues, under a gorget of bells and sleighbells that make her ribbed hair hum. The dimples, the elasticity of her cosy, connecting curves, the net of capillaries tinge her with blue and fan her, river teeming with fish, bread to roam in; the air, her vulnerable arms around the child, are fragrant.

The populous suburbs whistle, sound the alarm, as, above the factories, the fight-bombers, Caesarian of her belly, fly over, attack, tear to shreds, mutilate, wrench, and as the reproductive organs burst that she spits out, gravid.

She skims the cream from the milk with a ladle and moves it about, on her warm palms, and she tries to gather the gobs of fat from the cream so that little by little, the globs of butter grow then she drains the buttermilk and she kneads the salt dough to which she adds herbs, garlic, flowers, honey, onion and ham. The sparrows, the sky, the farm woman, protection for the lungs, shine, gorget, aroma, and the ringlets of the underbrush border the cabin and the milk cans.

Covered, she moistened her child with security, away from the call to mobilize, to shoot, to hit, that the armored, motorized, battle-scarred voices repeated below the other houses.

Above the ravaged zones, above the cemetery and trash coverings, what bridge, to ease her pain, will the child throw between her present of needs without hope and the mother, sifting flour near the cheeses, the young oxen, and the bucket, the mother who was smiling, near, still fuzzy, kittenish, fenced in by trellises, the grain fields shine, on her dappled dress, on her riding-hood and she sprayed, star spangled, the little hands, the little chubby buttocks looking for her in the hay.

People have gathered around her. They watch her bleed. They listen to her spurting blood boil. A few speak:
—Where is this blood coming from?
—Not from us, we are not bleeding.
—What is this blood?
—At home, the war is over.
—It's not doing us any harm. We don't feel anything.
—It's nothing to do with us, incomprehensible.
—Why does it spread so far?
—Who was she?
—Do something to get this blood under control.
—There is too much of it. It gets to you.
—Sensitivity becomes deadened.
—Clean off the sidewalks.
—Fetch some brushes, some boxes of detergent and pails of water.
—How can so much blood come out of only one victim?
—And who was killed more than a generation ago.
—And she has only one relative left. Why do we hear so many sobs?

—We think this spectacle of a dead female is disgusting.

—Flesh is not intelligent. It's not the flesh we must love.

—So much blood, it's all out of proportions.

—This blood is pushing it a little.

—It should hold back, show some control, dilute itself, intellectualize itself, abstract itself, instead of messing up our sidewalks.

—It's sordid, too plain, too raw.

—It's none of our business.

—From one organism to another, there is discontinuity and distance.

—It's our protection system, thank God.

—Otherwise, how could we carry on with all these other people in mourning, these wars, these unending catastrophes.

—Or, we would need to change everything.

—Enough talk! Quick, wash off our sidewalks.

(Reactionary, to come out of the need of you, to grow hard, to stop the voyage of exploration which, uselessly, calls out to you, and, to degenerate without resistance, without, from your flesh, where my heart still beats, never to try to build a renewed world?)

The little girl walks, inside the common forest, toward the carpenter's shop, through the coppices in the woods, the live oaks under coniferous trees whose dense tops shade and block her off from communication with the milk substance and there are rare clearings, a muscular rump, mottled with thickets and rain water where sinuous veins can be observed; the marblings of the muffle, of the belly near ground, crack, and the puddles, the reflections of the branches froth at the kidneys and the soft stray hairs, the veins standing out on the engorged teats, on the horns or on the leaves, lightly brush.

Surnames and first names, dates, flourishes of signatures, fingerprints, places of birth and of death in archives burned in the bombings, turn golden, turn pink the fumigations of the morgue whose bottles of antiseptic are lined up above the white sinks like baby teeth.

Gold from a retable and from twists, organs, ivory-like swell of the dough, stable, enamel, missal, in the warmth of the posts, she was

52

painting, she was adjusting her incense and stucco draperies in the backlighting of the rose windows where her train radiated.

How go on in these torsions of the blood on the move getting infected, the maggots are swarming, darkening, becoming covered with the flies of the bloody meat, itching, spoiling, gushing, engulfing, abusing, enraged, becoming inhuman, is no longer even the juice which was coming out of her quivering flesh with the tart odor of sacrifice?

Well stocked with spools of thread, the old women weave in front of the shanties. Region of trowels, of streams, of carpenters' shops, of stationery shops and of longevity, whose kitchens, redolent with loaves of bread and cheeses, smoke, near the hillsides covered with forests.

To touch you. To feel you. You are warm.

Sapped are the lapses, glaives, embers, the glaucous gluey glairs, pussy, glebe, tracked streaks where bodies contract and crack, that are transported and trucked, raucous rattles but nothing any longer is
oxygenated nor inflated with the beats and slow down, cease
a sigh rises from the military cemetery, crosses moors, peatbogs, layered swamps, the gullies of musculatures and climbs
on an underlinen stuck to the wood, sings, to the accompaniment of cymbals and triangles, chants terce, sext, none, vesper, compline, the terraced zones of vegetation, the oxen, the farmers, the deacons, the little columns and the arches of town squares, the canopy, the bread ovens, the waves of linen, the service of the morning incense, the service of the evening incense, the town shimmers, pages of communion and of meditation, canonical light, from which, on both shores of the river, the procession flushes up to the doors, up to the steep mountains, up to the horizon, up to the golden highlights of the flaring clouds.

The raisins, the dates from Cyprus and from Izmir, are washed, put in a large bin, and after three days, are mashed in a press. The juice thus obtained is put in large jars and used after forty days of fasting.

When, surrounded by the crosses and the wounds inscribed in the bread of the pressed cakes, the little girl wearing a hood of black cloth, under the thin marble arcatures, strokes the candle snuffer, the shoulders of the victims who, in funeral garb,

gasp and dribble, gashed by the flagstones,

and who are called out to by the little girl in tears

the dalmatic with stiff pleats, the shoulderbone, the breastbone, the ribs, the spine, the collarbones showing through the crimped linen, and in the center of the cuffs with filigreed braids the wristbone, the handbone, and the fingerbones hanging

and, run through the ring of a reliquary-clasp, the wimple cord circling, cold.

Balsam chips. Pine shade where the goats, the giant roosters, the tarragon, the tea basil, the chervil, the cider were soothing at the edge of the bedroom and the scrubbed wood knots, the pluvial pulp of a face that the mills powdered with flour.

Lattice, fluted bonnet, the roads look for your starching, your closets full of stacks of re-embroidered linen,

your cottage balconies with waxed and carved awnings your wheelbarrows on your skirt historiated like a mill town veiny with canals, with rivers where flow bunches of radishes, the timber, the quartered logs, the millstones, the hundred pound weights of grains,

Where the eyelet ruffles, the festoons of the looped drapes in the dressing rooms fattened the air, the villages, the cart-roads, the meadows of the trousseau

Which concealed, worker ant, in the rich soil erected in a dome-shape, by the winter of downpours and of clouds, you had satinstitched, you had hand hemmed, red ant, in front of the stained glass windows, under the pilot light of the tea kettle, under the gas pull-down lamp, hanging from a grooved moulding

From the depth of the cushions, your semolina hair, in the loss of light clothes the interior walls, lights up the panes of the high double windows.

The little girl turns her head toward the North, toward the West, toward the East, toward the South, begins to scream with all her might, is hungry, is thirsty, is hurting.

The coppices, the thickets, the waves, the clitoris of your flesh, ovary, clearing, your genital light springing up, laying, becoming grassy, golden, getting brighter, relaxing

No longer lives.

And on your fingernails, on the stained glass windows, on the eiderdowns of your bed of white wheat, above the waxed woodfloor and a mat of heather climbs the rambling image, in half-shade and protected from the wind, where the gluten seeds swell, where the gluten stretches, elastic, amid the gas and the steam bubbles, where the heat from the oven, blood temperature, penetrates the dough, where the gluten sets, where the sugars are caramelized in golden crusts, loft

And your soft dough remains moist.

And the bread was good.

And you reopen the field of your arms, and make the hustle and bustle of the crafts sing under the arches of the workshops

Urban cavity which a convex mirror reflects in a recess of the steel, in the back of the room, under a small opening for which the reflecting wall of a courtyard is the only source of light.

Through the glasses in the shape of bottle bottoms, the little girl makes out copper cauldrons, and a pewter mug hanging on the wall.

The horned furs protect against the cold. And the little girl wears herself out toward the snow-covered pines toward the wooden shoes; daily, a housewife waxes, toils (she is a lacemaker, cupboard, spinning-wheel, Flanders, kneading-trough, vaulted cellars, salt boxes, flour boxes, sideboard, earthenware pot); the old floor tiles carry the little girl toward the forgotten signs. The clouds produce calvaries, roofs, steeples, stone calendars, the image hangs the smoked herrings, the sausages, the lard, the salami on a stick, in the fireplace, just a few inches from the hearth.

But the mask, like a coffin, does not open, and howls bury in the mourning blocks, colonnades, scattered tambours of a column, funeral tower, stands, stela, hypogea. No mercy is given. She brings her hands up to her breasts. Shreds of intestine, of stomach, of liver, of pancreas, spurt blood. Next to the fatty cushion of the hip, the wad of a bun unwinds, victim lying on the ground: nurses from the Red Cross pick up the nursing mother with care.

The waves, the grass, the spindrift, the ebb writhes, sticks, swells, climbs, kelp, membrane, surrounds with breathing, rains on a gelatinous fishmarket, on a curling iron, on shrimping nets, mashes a bride's crown, flits in skylight or in evaporation, among the branches, among the gossamers, among the skeins, among the filaments, among the strands, among the coils, among the strings, among the ribbons, habitation, blondeness of thread where she is lit, where she is framed, where she weaves herself as though she were coming, Ash-blonde, very near me (may she enclose me with her whitening, with her crenelated ramparts, with her curtains, with her arms in ample perystilar sleeves!) to reside there, to weld me there.

Palpitate, vertically implanted, the dugs from which comes the milk, to fill the cans and for the production of butter, of the consistency of blocks beaded with drops of water and salty and fat preserved in stoneware, and in the milk room, for the production of hard or soft cheeses, covered with linseed oil, on the wooden table, fat curds, lean curds, cottage cheese, cream cheese, *coeur à la crème*, with shallots, tome of curds, kneaded, rubbed.

The glands of the nosegay coil up, cling to the lace insertion drenched with moisture, in a cot whose shadow drags across the ground, so that at dusk in the semi-consciousness, your sweetness will be preserved, town where the milk foam is kept, where corporations of manufacturers are organizing, are prospering, under the freckles, under the beauty spots, under the welts, under the ointment applied to the aureola and to the irritated nipple, and where the merchants, the craftsmen, the idlers, the printers under the wrought iron signs of the passageway, at the foot of the swollen mountains, come across the odors, the crust of the crisp hot croissants, golden. The inside, above the wares, the bridges and the piers, consists of a thick custard she lets ooze through the slats of the shutters; she works in a white apron, near the marbled stove; she stirs with her fingers, she spreads with the rolling pin, she lines the bottom of the pan with a layer of bacon slices and a layer of poultry stuffing, she tastes, she adds while stirring, the starch, the crests, the *quenelles*, the truffles to decorate the crust. And the Grand Canal, with the barges, with the tugboats, with the rafts, divides her, spreads out, lingers in meanders, weaves, flows, moves toward the shipyards where the cod, salty, gutted and cleaned, is drying in the sun, toward the trawlers, toward the floating nets, toward the shrimp beds, toward the bownets, and the Grand Canal penetrates her production of warmth, her lymph, her strands of arteries, of tiny vessels and of veins, the sanguinary showers, the sounds of her heartbeat, her flowing system, her gallons of blood, the breathy smile of her lungs, of her skin, the day's pulse overloaded with iodine, with ozone and with radioactivity, and my strengths circulate like men's healing, when you will come to take the place of indifference and cold, that you will constantly come, that you will constantly meet us and that you will gather us together and, that, having freed yourself of the unknown with which the war, the impotence, the violence of the world cover you, I will finally be able to gaze at you, and after this long, patient, hesitating, anguished, sobbing call of my system in pain, to attempt to revive the massacred motherly light, by becoming one with it, by feeding on it, by imitating it, by reaching beyond individuality, without getting tired of cherishing you so

the child's little hand clutches, gluttonous, the neckline of the absent woman.

During the perspiration of the nap, the sand, blond siliceous, detrital, nude, piles up in masses, in dunes, goose bumps, around the tits, under the eddies of the dry wind, grows, hardens, fills out spreads in a brassiere, fills it, overflows, is swollen, is ground down, then necrophagous, I move away. I walk. I pass through villages where the skin texture, frosted, exposed to the sun, incandescent, among the potsherds, suffocation, darts, twirls, rough coats of the walls, into alleys, into razor blades, into spirals, into spasms, without shade, without exit. I am thirsty.

The continental winds create sand storms without ever bringing rain to the uniformity which, over great distances, exiles, wrinkles, uses up

I walk as though I were immobilized, as though I were struggling.

Under the tripod, under the ladder, under the two benches, under the stool of a retreat, the washwater breaks. The bark, the tannin, the pockets of strong smelling resin, the treetops, the guipure rinsed, wrung dry, enter through the nostrils, facing the clearing, facing the ford whose gallons of leaves and buds raise, expand the chest.

I try to breathe in.

I drag myself over the images of my torment, over my inability to draw the resemblance, and as I try to imagine this mother, I realize that I do not see her, that I do not hear her, that I do not smell her scent, that I do not touch her, that I do not taste her — that there is no one. My senses cannot grasp her, cannot inspire this despair and this love that I feel, with the organs of a shifting, dim, immense body where you might swarm

And only, maybe, to bleed until I rot, will return me to you; to infiltrate, to stuff your humidity, your compost, your warmth, your darkness, to cram them, with a continuous discharge, the viscous, red, tart, salty roots, hemorrhage, which will circulate among your particles, will explore you, and will once again pull me in with you.

(Because here in these metallic, masculine and futuristic zones, you are as invisible as the veins on a corpse.)

III. *Mausoleum*

Glory be to her, Praise, Honor to the strewing of shade.

The height winds in a spiral.

I cover the remains, I divide myself, I increase on my shudders, on the rosaries of ganglions, on the flaccid of her veins, on the clots, on the darkness of her walled-up mouth to which, like skin on the skeleton of a live woman, I cling.

"Identify us with the fog driven by her crypts into the depths of the hillsides, with pointed arches, which, through the wine from the vials, from the stills and from the alembics, drift. But sometimes we are illuminated by the oriflamme of the sun on the cartographic light of the miniature manuscripts whose waves, fires, azure, egg yolk beam, halo. We turn crimson, we sparkle, we bubble, facing the semicircular arches, the bas-reliefs, the vaults, the cornices, the capitals, where the sculptures climb and the clusters, fitted like pack saddles on a donkey, the borough's fortifications, barrels and the virgin in her apron filled with grape seeds, holding in her hand vine shoots and the steeple overlooking the earth where, wearing a hooded coat, the vinegrower prunes and digs, glow, unfold, like a streamer and vines whose twinklings, tangles, initials, capitals, historiated characters, among the pillars, light us, to such an extent that instead of a chasuble and a mitre, we wear the luminous vibrations of the purple radiations and the red radiations, bygone day which, transfusion, dimples in the blood-red cheeks, baby button-faces, foam, warm . . . "

Her gildings, like a clearing adhere to the roughcast, adorn with escutcheons, stars, blazons, crowns, diadems, fleur-de-lis.

The leaf's throbbing.

The difficulty in the breathing stems from the water vapor across the pedestals. Pulmonary incense, a taper, the rattles, under the subfoundations, burn.

I feel my way through the pages.

Paper, the rags, the crested dress, vellum, pulped, parchment, skin, reduced to a paste outside the margin rise in a cloud of dust, I play with papers, I get discouraged.

Dark smears stain, I wrinkle the shapeless and colorless deceased, the crêpe floss, the silk cope whose fripperies are draped, the loose fabric of the black ink.

Behind the buttresses and the moats, the spirals, the circles, the zigzags, the signatures front and back become superimposed, become condensed, seal up with lead.

I stroll about.

The grain, the tone, the patina of a list of names dig, hew, carve, prop up, vault.

Combustion where naked torsos and the wheat bent toward the ground crumble, brighten with sunshine, interkiss, in the limestone, panting where the frieze revives, where the arcades are spelled, inscribe themselves, geometrically construct themselves in capital letters, round themselves in uncial letters, where, laminated, the breath of the book, the architecture of the strokes vermilion the blocks, the grooves, the school desks, where the mica and the quartz spangle the granite of the walls.

She filters in, oozes, dilutes, buckles, crackles, shimmers, flakes, soaks, frizzes, gurgles, wrinkles, settles, rots, blanches, rusts, erodes.

I compile, I decipher.

And the departed pallor absorbs oil like a wick and scorches the parchment and spreads; fumes whose gothic letters line up; leaves where, among the first names, the gold mingles, weaves, sputters, public records, charters, notary deeds, gospel-books, stocks, chronicles throwing flames. And caught in the solid mass or else lodged in the blisters of the glazing or else placed in the extra thickness or else tossed in the holes, she pours the glimmers.

I examine. I bump into the rock.

crisscross, record, bend, place of refuge, its features with the posthumous proportions of monuments, their resistance, their cathedrals, their nuggets, their strength, their permanence, which transfigure, put throbbing rhythm into the decomposition, the precariousnes. (But fail to draw to themselves, our desire to press against the chest which, outside of earth, liberates its energy, confuses us, calls in our abandoned bodies.)

Life becomes rarefied, sheds its leaves, freezes, - 200 ºC, - 270 ºC, - 337 ºC, - 350 ºC, - 338 ºC, I move forward, desolation, frigidity, hibernation, coma, the vastnesses become impoverished, get worse, the temperature keeps dropping. It is cold, always colder: -398º C. I shiver, caught by the ice. Glacial silence! Absence! There remains only a naked winter, a surface covered by an ice cap with no solar disk above the horizon and I also, I degenerate, I become exhausted, I lose weight, I contract, I will waste away, I will dwindle, I will darken, I will move away, I will disappear, mixed in with the uniformity of this stillness, of this hardness, of this night, of this chill.

Oh! Where are we to seek refuge? How to extricate ourselves from devastation? from desolation? from the string of mistakes? from the ruins of flesh? from annihilation? What did we do to lose the taste of the earth-mother? But let us move on toward her! so we can at last be allowed to love, to cross over into the zone of love . . .

MOTHER EARTH
(LA REVERIE)

Mother Earth

Pieces of vertebrae, molars whose enamel is incomplete, a portion of forehead with brow ridges, fragments of a femur, of a tibia, of a fibula, cranial fragments with the fontanel still gaping, a brainpan, a face with prominent nasal bones, long bones of feminine appearance, animal remains, the crown of a molar half calcified, the chin hole, an upper maxillary whose teeth fell out possibly post-mortem, a whole skull, almost nothing left that can be reconstituted, identified under the graves among which you walk, you walk, searching for her . . .

"In the days when Berthe was weaving" . . .

I would polish the floor with a wool skate; I would wash the bath marbles with soft soap and I would rub with pumice-stone. The heaviness of my shirt-warmer breasts would weigh me down.

The weather was beautiful and the child would unpleat its lungs outside my womb so it could bloom, so it could sprout. The diapers would overflow in the wash boiler.

I loved this cuddliness enriched by the good yogurt of the flesh, from which, curdled, tickled, the cellulite would burst out laughing, right where the tufted dimples, among the furbelows and the ankle socks would quilt the knee joints like little cushions. Hair would curl on this daintiness; it would come out of me, would brush lightly, would scatter, soft, soft, soft, in the light of day, through her prattle, through her beauty spots and through her freckles, daughter of inflorescence where would twirl gossamers as though my motherhood, during my pregnancy, had grafted her on a hawthorn hedge.

I, bread-eater, would watch over, from the window, the acres.

I was knitting pink wool booties for the baby.

In the stairway would fly, would chirp, borrowed from the sun, the light into which, coming from darkness and death, I would rise, where, on each landing, whiteness would lean its rays, would reflect, would enclose the birds with a torrid urn whose porcelain, on the seventh floor, under the rafters, I would go across up to, insolation, zenith, our room with a southern exposure where you would arouse my rotation, my orb, you would greet me like the East, like the triumph of day over night, like the spring equinox, and, resurrection, you would dart, would brighten me, you would initiate me and the furnace would pour its glitter on top of me, you would tingle, you would tire me, you would cover me with blisters, you would blush me, you would dry my tongue, I would undress in eruption, I was hot, I was thirsty.

Already with my eyes I would admire your athletic build, the hardness of your virile member, its circumference. And, in your arms, for the husband, for the tree, for the harvest, I would link myself to a jerky motion, to a long channel, similar to the vagina of a cow in heat whose period through the secretion of the clitoris and the lips of the vulva, lubricates. I was naked, subject to instinct, a servant to life. I was straddled by the bundle of hairs and bristles. He would lay me down. He would push, under the rush of blood. He would come out of his sheath. He would stuff me. He would fasten me to him. Oh! marriage of voluminous testicles, he would penetrate my chamber, he would penetrate, fully, my entrails. He would bring me abundance, sprinkling. The commissures, the nostrils of your bites would fill my mouth with saliva and beard. In you, I was sheltered from hunger, I was invigorated, and like water in the ground, I would circulate. The swelling would anoint with red clay my obesity and would blow, would transport us from one continent to the other, from one hemisphere to the other, from one solstice to the other. Your hands, your excitement, would taper me in the shape of pearls, of galaxies, would swell me with reefs, down to my belly, at the center of the earth foaming with seas and oceans where the undergarments that you had taken off me, would float, would embroider the currents, the wind, the air, the dust, and would disappear and your member like the salty waves, would break into foam, would rub on the bottom, would swoop forward, would spread out in a layer of well-being, would enlarge my opening, would dig into me, would strike me, would roll me, would shake me under its blows, would expand exaggeratedly, would divide into arms, into legs which would encircle me, would climb back up to my tongue, would tie me up, would be wound around me, would lick me, would press me against him, against his chiseled cliffs, parted by the spine, under my fingers, oh fusion whose pressure would squeeze me, whose speed would zigzag, would become more pronounced, would clear away, would toss me, would cart away my pearly tremors, would flood me with ebullitions, would gully me while tingeing me with his dark eyes.

The thighs, the buttocks, the breasts would rise up like a new chain of mountains. The resin, the gum would exude. We were a hasty return in the colostrum, in the union where lava, matter, cereals, outflow, dough, paté, silt, ejected, would thicken, solidify, obstruct the suckling orifice; bubbles, masses, hot gas-jets, would explode, granules of your cheeks, of your ill-shaved chin, would scratch me, would smother me, my spasms would sketch themselves around you, would wrinkle the magma. I would crumble. The space between your body and mine, let us fill it, bind yourself to me, even if I do not know who you are, what you are, what is left of you, of me, come from the kernel of the earth, descend from the strata, the rocky bark as we come together, gluttons, pioneers, vertebrates, in search of new lands to clear, to sheave, to shape.

The fluid's nucleons, without disturbing their cohesion, were moving about.

The temperature would rise, would transport me toward the red zone of the specter.

It was no longer dark.

I would mold, would work with my hands, knead, fashion, malt, massage, mash, bolt, butter, brew.

Ruddy . . .

Atoms, molecules, colloidal aggregates, chyme.

Mother-ores, shapeless material in a melted state, this porridge as it cooked, would stick, curdle, billow, dilate, occupy the empty space, would lead to the construction of a universe, "it's dripping," to its relief, to its concentric aureoles, to its twists and turns, to its puckerings, to its pads, to its depressions, to its sides where, in certain places, were inserted muscles which, pinched, caressed, under the hairs, would contract, to your hail pebbles falling on me, to the thunder, to the lightning of our organs come into contact, you would electrify me, your fleece would crackle, your energy would spend itself in the form of fires and lightning bolts.

The embers would smoke.

The cinders would swim at the surface.

You would paw the plump dough nested, ignescent in my shirt. I would bubble, proteins, plasticity at the confines of extensibility. I would become dented, mamillated, disarrayed, corpulence of the terrain. I would let you, beyond health, reach the crust, arrive at the lentigo, at the ganglia, at the comedos, at the buboes, at the folds, at the acne. You would steal forth, cuddle under the nylon, you would unhook, right where the fat smelled bad, ballooned, bagged, bundled, where, replete, I would swell again, where the pus collected, where the pustules, the papules, proliferated in these regions of the skin, of the flesh, which, hidden by underwear, are deprived of air and sunshine, are sausaged in but, freed, spread in pendulous mammae, in rounded belly, in pubis, quivering. The fatty acids, deposited in my adipose tissues would flavor. I would fidget. I would become sticky. You would thrust your hands, your penis toward the most flabby parts where you would munch, would spread my edges apart, would penetrate my vagina, explore me, visit me in details, poke me to such an extent that you would find yourself caught in my viscera like in the mines, like in the depths of the earth still at work, the hearth, the veins, in order to, underneath this, reach, loaves of fire, kernel of liquid steel, solid rock from the center, what excess of heat? I would bubble, brown, crunch, smoke. You would knead, in the pout, in the flaccid, in the moistness, in the puffiness, in the witherings, in the fibers of this soft dough which, turned out of its girdle and its brassiere, would adhere to you everywhere, would pucker, which you could not unglue from yourself, would collapse, chubby, under your weight, without getting flatter, without getting thinner, "don't ever leave me again, don't ever leave me again!" would drag you, would set you ablaze one the reverse side of the surfaces, would inspire in you its fanned, ash-blondeness.

The luminous sign would light in true red the room, would transform it into ambient meat where, titillated, teased, my organs from which you squeezed the juice, would become red, would gain in homogeneity, would become tender, would flutter.

I would writhe.

And under the balcony, at an altitude, the town with the cloudy sky, were bulbs, cupolas, roofs, terraces, observatories, telescopes, radiotelescopes in which flickered, in which mushroomed the window panes.

You would massage me, perched on top of my mountains of fleshiness. You would stretch your muscles taut and you would press. We would intermingle, we would abolish the evolution of life, we would return to a beginning, to the primitive midst from which we could no longer be distinguished: carbonized and nitrogenous compositions falling like rain from the atmosphere, mineral salts, acids, bases, particles of mud contained in a solution in which to assemble, bony, nervy, lymphatic, the cells, in which to form its tissues.

Diffuse, you would emanate from daylight, would pass through my depth, through my hearth, through my protuberances, would go down to the bottom, would chase away the darkness, it was sultry, stormy, would render me diaphanous.

Nudity would appear to the rhythm of its allures, would become ordered, organized, would increase in size under my tight-fitting summer dress. You would undress me with a look.

And, dozens of miles from here, were being scrubbed interiors of extra fine butter around which the undulations, in the sun, were creamy with cow tits, while in basements, below the vegetable ground, were mildewing, were felting the cheeses of these doughy, unctuous villages, on which one could subsist.

"What are you pawing?" I would become limber, mammal, oily arborization, gluteal fold, bunch of muscular fibers, lying raw under the sheet: "what is it? do you speak? are you someone? a signal?" The consumer, without answering, would kiss my morsels, would feel my tenderness, would appreciate my freckliness, my dappleness. It was good. My redness would make him cry. I was fragrant. The hues of my sensitivity, under the rouge were born of a face with features more delicate, he would say, breathing me in, than the capillary vessels. And having stripped my front bare, he would feel the weight of my breasts, would rumple, owing to pigments analogous to those of an egg yolk and animal fat, the blondeness which abounded on the lard of my back, on the dubbin of my fifth quarter, on my rump, between my two hips and on my enormous hams; and the pulpy dough would no longer lose its puffiness, roast beef, veal shank, thigh, slices, wet-nurse, round steak, leg of lamb of my flesh which he grabbed by the handful, filet mignon into which he dug his fingers, "woman, woman . . . " he would say; pink gums, long nipples, healthy teeth, she would smile while giving herself to the distension; her lips, to inhale, would move like a pump, woman, woman whose waist is smaller, whose loins are deeper, whose temperature is lower than the man's, softness whose surface, at the tip of the breast, becomes rough with tubercles, her breasts would keep on swelling, growing, flesh-colored, wild, satiny, liliaceous, bluish red, purplish, roseate white, blooming, palissé, plumed, protean, poppy, crimson, blood-red, flushed, large size, and as a result of the milking, were foaming, casting the milk afar, while bursting their sac, were gorging, flowing, masses of comforting and generosity, which could not be unbanded, could not be defatted, fat slice, fat vein, gristle, first foot, second foot, double chin, double fat, mardi gras, shortening, sinewy tenderloin, tender-tender, shoulder of beef, shoulder of ham of her mellow, would produce large waste, would stock the cold storage installations, the butcher's blocks, the counters, the scales on mattress, bolster, wholesale meat markets so that crammed, the man got a mouthful and from his elbow to his stifle, he would savor the belly trouncing the stock-piled pants, the leather against which, dark, swarthy, his scrotum would bend, to grumble, to brood, while she would get fatter, while she would provide for him, while she would excite his appetite, while she would become invaginated, the back side solidly built, the edge of the anus purple red, as her price would go up, while her value in the butcher's trade would become confirmed, while you would chew me, while I would reconsitute myself, leg, spine, sirloin, T-bone, haunches, rib steak, eye of the leg of lamb, loin chop, eye of round, rumploin, scrag taking in the salt well, rare, setting the fat and I would heap fat on you, you would grate me, grind me without your getting satiated, center of breast, large chunk of breast, hind quarter, Charolais, midrump, that you would palpate, pinch, pat, blade, shoulder of juiciness, of enjoyment, of freshness, on which, in front of the fold, you would graft your breeches, where you would work my meat, where, in your mouth, you would reduce me to a state of soft lard and of blood, and, meat, I would fill your digestive track and you would push me toward your gullet, toward your pharynx, toward your stomach, toward your intestines, and I would pass through your vessels, we were one and the fibers would get together to form primary bunches, would gather to form secondary bunches then tertiary bunches and finally these muscles to which love would bring oxygen, I was attached to you, we could no longer be told apart, the water would link itself to us, would take charge of us, we would hypertrophy, we would get out of breath: "don't leave me, don't leave me" and my thirty ounces of tongue would wet you down to the egg of our moistness and you would suck me, distort me, mince me, your teeth would penetrate my damp, my sexual odor, urine, sweat, female hormones, you would plunge into my meaty, into my carcass, into my disjointed ham, into my rind, into my well fleshed-out neckline, you would cuddle me, you would sniff me, it was necessary to go lower, lower, before History, dig, prospect ourselves, search ourselves, progress into the flesh like the root into the ground, pull the truth, from the darkest, the most vulgar, the most animal levels in ourselves, derive thanks, rediscover respect, the ceremony of life, the amazement of functioning, the amazement of beating, eternally, in the heart of the world. And, incontinent under the effects of mastication, I would yield my juice and the man's gluttony would compress my fibers and, from jowls to pasterns, my build would become plump, would give the maximum of satisfaction on my succulence, on the luminosity of that color that the man, driven mad, would crush, slice, perforate, shear, without being able to calm down and I would mingle with the juicity of your palate, it was necessary to move forward into the water, into the nitrogen, into the myofibrillae, into the myoglobin, into the collagen, into the glycerides, into the glycogenes, into the acidity, into the extensibility, into the sarcoplasma of the muscles, move forward into the lard, into the small fat of the adiposity, move forward into the interstitial liquid, into the gelatin, into the loose elastin, into the packages of conjunctive, the man would move forward without being able to stop, I would beautify, would press him against me, with gratitude, closing my eyes, and you would plunge into my buttocks, into my fleshy panicle, into my large ancon, into my trappings, and, under, inter, intra me, you would woo me, you would grip me, freed from the suffering and from the solitude, finally! finally! And a gynecologist would be able to see uterine horns rich in normal embryos and yellow substances on each ovary and she was capable of depositing some fat, fat in her erogenous zones for the production of pounds of live weight, on each side of the backbone, behind the shoulder, as the kisses pass by, at the level of the last rib, and equidistant from the stifle and from the back of the ham, and the man would flatter her with his hand and would lay her right on the mass of mountains, topography of fish bones and bumps whose flesh and breasts the man would seize by fistfuls, no longer knowing where would begin the mineral kingdom, where would begin the animal kingdom of the salients and of the cavities that he was thus exploring with his hands, she would become fidgety, an increase in

71

blood pressure was taking place in her aggravated by the acceleration of the cardiac rhythm, her arterioles would burst, dotting her with red blotches; the meat fibers, the film of fat located on the fibers would decompose the light coming in from windows of her insides which were becoming iridescent, where the bright pink, the dark red, the light red, the whiteness would shine, through the stream, would flow, would bleed, menstruation, menorrhagia releasing a sticky odor where the dry man would become soaked, where he would penetrate into the parts infiltrated with fat and in the muscles, up to the bone marrow where he would spread himself out through the quivers and she, feverish belly, she would moan to call, to feel again, and the man would dissolve the plasmic membrane, would penetrate the cell, and the cell would become larger, divide, form new cells which would divide, which would take on a blue coloration, the woman would hold him, hold him tight, he would spill her pieces of fat and of lean meat, would shake her, would penetrate her through her pores, she would pant, she would whisper: "I feel good, I feel good." Nothing of themselves was foreign to them anymore; the surge of energy would regenerate them, would reanimate them everywhere. And we would blend into each other and prime matter, the fat matter would come closer to the mimicry of a human being with two heads, concretion uneven, compact where, subcutane-ous, the sun, the moon, the stars would give us their light, would penetrate deeply into the interior of the muscular tissue, would purify, would vivify, I would sigh while opening up, while revealing a mass of breath between my lips, stretching, virginity, air torsion, I would kiss you, mouth-to-mouth, crater, atmosphere where you, your lungs inter-mingled in mine, you would get swallowed up, promising me never to be apart from me again, from this inside which was freeing you. She would sob. At first localized at the surface of the rubbing, the pleasure would beam over the whole abdomen, and, erected, her clitoris, the innumerable nerve endings, the corpuscles of voluptuousness would adhere to the dorsal side of the penis, would perceive the size of the caliber, she would love, she would adore, half-reclining, her legs folded, she would apply a suction on the penis, she would feel clasped, something, gradually, would approach, would manage to insert itself, would creep inside her, compressing her on the right and on the left, would gather strength, would be ejaculated, which she would reject with the acidity of the vagina and which she would inhale, which she would detain, which she would push into her cervix with the help of the spasmodic contraction of her muscles, and, outside the prostate, and the seminal vesicles, the sperm would run, and its streams luminous like the solar systems, would flow into themselves, would go across her and, agile, the spermatozoids would climb, would reach her uterus, her tubes and, having reached the level of the ovary, the spermatozoids, inside the ovule, would fill her with immortality, would transmit the features, would abolish wear, would continue lineage, would reproduce me, would reproduce us, genes carriers of pigment, carriers of sex, carriers of species, would return to the stock, to the kernel, to the zygote, and the chromomeres splitting in two, each chromosome would head toward a pole, and the gametes would meet, get together, order the type, message descended from parents and from grandparents, would unite, would participate, cells, would multiply, in the genealogy that I would dredge with schist, would surround itself with continents, with islands and with archipelagos bound together by the blood, would populate the mountains, I would exploit organic and continuous and impossible to differentiate matter, and my large lips hiding the small ones, under the turfing of the pubis, would become infiltrated with fat, would become firm, and my nipples would point, and from my structural superpositions, from my reflexes, from my bifurcations, from my heightenings, from my complications, from my curves, from my uneven levels, from my intricacies, life would be derived, "my love." I would flare, I would gape, orifices, yawns of ligaments and hemorrhoids where you would travel, your fingers, your fingernails, your skin, your foreskin, "my darling, my darling", "touch, take everything." My flaccidity, my links, my cords, my vestibule, my veins, my filaments, my walls, my nerves which would encircle you, which would incorporate you in this well-built, in this boned dough of meat, coarsely ground, with reddening salts, with pierced hymen, with portions of fat, in this hypergenital woman whose secretions, transudation, serosity would facilitate your penetration, without your becoming sated with the plump roundness of her shoulders nor with that of her thighs nor with the good behavior of her fat, nor with the abundance of her meat, nor with the pink of her lardass intercoastal gaps, would tallow you and she would manufacture herself, dough, stuffing, hash, kidneys, tonsils and you would climax, with reptations, with palpations, her intestines, the small intestine, the colon, up to the anus where, crossing her arteries, you would double up, you would innervate yourself with her corpulence, with her underside, with her handles and she would flinch would scratch you, increasing to the point of paroxysm her activity, her preparation, popliteal, aponeurosis, iliopsoas, loin, sirloin where, membranous, tendinous, you would become entangled endlessly, shamelessly, would peck at her, kiss her, infraspinous, infrastructure, while entering the compression of her fibers, the bleeding of her red, would keep her in your arms, a long time, a long time, "my little one, my little one . . . ." You were reveling. The tips of her breasts, her boobs, "give yourself up freely . . . " your mouth, without holding back, would pulp them, would tear at them, the milk would wed itself to the crevices, to the chaps, you would harvest, you would gather, you would bring in bulk, you would stock your ration, "my precious, my dumpling" who would give in, would offer you no resistance, would let you eat your fill, "more, more . . . " suck the fibrillae, the spots, the surplices, the stratification, the pleating, the furrows, the striation, the folding where, with the first bites, you would rediscover the glands connected to the maternal principle of nature, like the earth, and her fat meat would look good on her, touch her volumes, sculpt their fat, plant yourself in the depilated flesh where brown red lines, on the tracks of your teeth, would appear; and she would put everything on the outside, you would pinch her between the thumb and the other fingers, you would run your hand over her buttocks scratchable to the nail, you knew how to shape her, you would mould her under your fingers, your thumb would penetrate the hollow of her flank, would try to plunge between the muscular masses of the fattest, the most affectionate parts, to enter the compartments, appetizing, I would reinstate content and sense to physiological gestures, I would reveal to you a rite, something other than me, a sacrament of rumen, of pluck, of crunch, of guts, and the red meat would connect us to each other like the bones of a ribcage on a slab of beef, and for hours, she would keep you reclining in her water retention, in her fibrous tumor, in her consistency where, in the process of savoring, you would become more human: "my wife . . . my wife . . . ," it was your own lungs adhering to my trachea, and, integrated with my body, you would function through my convolutions, through their number, through their ordering, through my interstices, through my sinuosities, through the raised shapes produced by my veins, and, as if begging you to continue, I would whisper, guiding your hands over me: "yes, yes . . . yes." around my navel, higher, lower, everywhere. And I would shrink below so as to hold you tighter, to encase you better, and you would pull me across the thread of my meat, and my ligaments, my nerves would bend to you in the flexures, in the elbows, in the cul-de-sacs, would crowd in your mouth, and my first cuts would be retailed in slices, would answer with their juice, with their vermilion, "delicious, delicious . . . ." And as though watching over me, you would pass the palm of your hand over me, over the receptivity, over the irritability, over the vulnerability of this flesh which nothing preserves, but from which, passionately, you would foresee that, even after death, I would continue to emanate, to illuminate, as long as at the heart of the physico-chemical unity of the world, there will be love, there will be amazement. Her gaps, her fissures, her fractures were filled, the helter-skelter, couples changing, overflowing, pumice, fumaroles, limestone, carapace, offals, sima gravel, eruptive panspermy, would envelop you like a jewel box, siliceous with corns, with cañons, with volcanoes, with cirques, with chilblains, with callosities, with channelings, and you would grab hold, without letting go, you would bury yourself in it, you would get bogged in it, you would solidify in it, you would crystallize in it, you would bespatter yourself in it "I enervate you, I enervate you . . . " you would hand yourself out to her mountain-ous, to her uterus, to her vagina, through afferent, efferent branches, through twigs, through ramifications, through nets and in her you would branch off, you would evacuate, thickness, abundance, flexuous cork, ropy, viscous, sensitive, which she could barely stand "you're mine, you're mine . . . ." You would possess her, enlarge her waist, plug her up, force her to yell: "ouch! ouch!", would forage her, burrow her, harrow her, blotch her, nothing left of her to resist in this substance, in this gift each of whose summit would rise, would become sharp, would form a point, would flocculate, would unite, balancing you, relieving you, ruling over your health, revealing to you your own flesh. "who is it? where am I? so much, so much?" Her large breasts, her large sensuals, at whose level your mouth would be located, you would seize them together, in their totality, keeping your lips pressed against the areola, and never satiated, you would squeeze the nipple between your lips, you could not contain yourself anymore, you would release your energy, to the maximum, and she would flow in clear, bluish, translucid gutters, "my salty one . . . " and you would let yourself be invaded by her kindness which would make your childhood surface as though you had really

75

come back to the source, been put out to nurse. She was still without stability, still like the preformal modality of matter, like a regression into the amorphous; nothing structured would arise from out of her yet, but, if pregnant, she would spread herself out in all directions, and her softness could be recovered, repeated, and the embryo would inherit her softness, how loving she was! malleable young woman, inhabitable where a child would settle down, build its residence, how you would find her soft! She would recognize you at your skin stretched by the muscles, at the vibration of your effort, and, above, at your receding hairline, at that place of yours where her hands, with timidity, with respect, could touch your temples, your mind, and submissive, she would let you organize her being, make yourself her master, find her, she would sob, "I can't live without you, I can't live without you . . . " her flesh would jump, become impregnated with you. She would beg you: "again! again!" she would wait, you would look each other in the eyes, her eyes were like the planetary skies, like a sort of fluid, like a sort of beyond which abolishes anguish and you would flee in the contemplation of their grandeur, in the shape of their lines, in their variations of colors, in their cloudy rearranging, in their layers of clear and shady, in their lay-out of alternating beds of blinkings and of silence, in the confusion of this blue . . .

When you come out of her, it is dark. You stagger. The cold of the street. You are once again alone. That's it. A man, once again, defenseless. Once again, this incomplete existence. Uneasy. A man out in the street. A man of no importance. And once again, this pity. And the certainty that there is no solution . . . you walk, you walk . . . that the threat prowls.

Her flesh, her instinct, from so much purity would become a collective flesh, the people, the breathings, the reserves of vitality of the world, when so much truth, so much well-being, would last, would last in your arms, more imperative than a law, than a moral code, than a religion, this flesh of peace, this flesh of love, which would send you its breath, and which would soften you on contact, you would stroke it, you would caress it with contemplation, you would enter it beyond words, beyond the visible, to the deepest, where death, where destruction can no longer penetrate, and in a low voice, you would call out "my soul, my soul . . . " while you would hole up in the image of this face.

You wanted to guess, could not strike her from your future. No one would be able to influence, to complete more carnally than she, the physical, earthy dialect of physiognomy, of your abrupt, harsh type, with marked features, natural extension of the tormented region where isolation, dejection had united you both, where, in your surroundings, the roads, analogous to the lines of the hand, would furrow the mountains, the juttings like your palms and would constitute what premonitions? what signs? You would fight fate for her. You would jostle her. You would beat her: "promise me, promise me, swear to me . . . ", "give us time to . . . ." And the unknowable in her and in you, would exasperate you, you were so afraid of being without her, of being left empty, of having her taken away from you.

The sun set, the flesh would turn silver in the moonlight, and in your gratefulness at being together, you would proclaim yourselves capable of facing the trials of the stay on earth, to assume the brevity of this stay. Yes, the obstacle, it was this human condition, but I could not get used to it, even if your body, mortal, precarious, had not stopped reminding me of it, opposing its limits disproportionate to my love for you. And each night, before going to sleep, I would huddle against you, I needed to verify that you were there, still there: "are you breathing? you're breathing? you have not stopped living? you don't hurt? there, vigorous, intact for how much longer? how much time? how much time do we have left? . . . "

"No! no!" He would pull her against him, against his bulging fly indicating a state of tumescence: "stop! stop! . . . " Her lips would part, she would sigh contentedly, no longer attempting to escape the hold of the senses, the heat flashes, and the skin casing would burst, just like the little leaves of buds from which, coaxed, would assert themselves, would break loose her forms, the rotundities of her body of which she was losing control, and her defenses would snap like pants one wants to remove too fast, and, ready, her nudity would give itself over to the man, to sensuality. They would fit each other exactly, imbedded in the warm, in the narrow, one in the other, succeeding in fashioning a sort of mucous refuge, where, under the blankets and the sheet, they felt far from danger, and where their contortions would merge: "you make me lose my head . . . you make me lose my head! . . . " she would spread, moving them, her legs signaling powerlessness in taming this excess, these shocks dominating her to the extent that she would become unconscious. And the man, erect in her, would ask: "you like that? it's good?", "do I do this to you? I go on?" she would acquiesce with a gluey groan.

After, for a while, she would be restored, as though, from life, she had just obtained a surplus of strength which could postpone, would weaken, could lessen the effects of wear and death.

Rubbed, this part grown ten times its size because of the rubbing, was more and more attractive to the muscular man who would stretch himself on it, would stiffen himself on it, she would deny him none of her nooks, none of her walls, she would have torn herself to make the way easier for him, he would climb down between her thighs, link by link, weaving: "I like this . . . I like this . . . " she would whisper, he would reach, thanks to the lengthening of the penis, the bottom, and would touch the womb, while above, the extreme flexibility of the feminine neck would mime the reflections, the plays of light, as she would be born, as she would disappear, as she would be born again, inciting him to follow her, to ask for her, to ardor: "I love you, I love you . . . " to surpass himself, to relive, as new after winter as the flowers on the fruit trees, when the sun, leaving the celestial southern hemisphere, moves toward the northern hemisphere, in the spring, at budding time, whose pink, this generous chest, this young woman had: "my country girl . . . ," "my simplicity . . . " which would bring him back to the basic elements: to butter, to salt, to dessert, to water, to oil, to milk, to bread, to primitive meat, to the oral stage when food had not yet lost its maternal fruitiness, "my beloved . . . my life."

The blinds in their room were not down. The moon, star born of the earth, millions of years ago, would pour in. The continents would bar the way to the tides. The child's first word was: Mama! The species were reproducing, even if death were succeeding life, and the fruits were ripening, and the cycle were never interrupted. The world was in order.

She would breathe regularly. The blood would arrive at the right auricle, would come back at the left auricle.

You promised you would take care of her. You would be faithful to her. You would handle her hypersensitivity carefully.

You believed in what does good, in what keeps warm, and you would repeat: "thank you, thank you, thank you" without understanding.

"My cream . . . ." Undressed, the cottony cozy, this body warmth which would shiver, which you would take in your arms.

The earth was turning through space.

The myriad stars were so high, so high! Venus, on the right, was sparkling with a reddish flash. You would have wanted to lose yourself. No matter that there were billions of years left, no matter that you would shout at the top of your voice, that you would cling to her, hold her in your arms, cover her with your body, warm her with your breath, she would eventually move away, she would eventually leave.

And you would imagine the brain in such a tender, soft gray, in the cranial box, and you would watch carefully her fits of coughing, her headaches, her little aches, her pulse, the sound of her breathing. You would panic. You would never forget how, for each one of us, transitory is the triumph of the blood circulating, of the heart beating . . .

"Let me admire you . . . ." Fatigue, sleepless nights would bring circles under her eyes, would make her look drawn: "you're happy!" The full moon would light the plants in the room, would cast gleams, under your caresses, would imprison you in her blond mystery where clouds would float. Infinite sky, without answer . . .

She would reconstitute herself, she would reshape herself, she would display her wares, her cellulite, she would slide under your fingers, you would give yourself over to her curves, to her skin texture, to her fleshed out shoulders, to her colorless down, you would unbutton her pajama top to uncover the breasts, globes of glands, of fat, of quivers where you would bite hungrily, where you would irritate enough to bleed, the red and hard erectile of each nipple; there, there, she would pant against you, all arched, all alive, your half, your cherished, your wife, you had your hands full.

But to the infrareds, to the ultraviolets, to the X rays, to the radiophonic waves, to the cosmic rays, the radium rays, the eyes are not sensitive, and she was like all the lights of this world we cannot see and you would feel you did not have sufficient support from all your senses to reveal her presence, that she would elude you, too vast, even in the embrace . . . "my love . . . ," that your bewildered, hungry arms could not hold her . . .

And being careful not to mess it up, you would bend over her hair where the combination of hair spray, shampoo and cologne, the arrangement of her hairdo, of this vaporous architecture, wavy, of her curly strands, of the blind arcatures of her tresses, of her spit-curls tiered from her ears up to her wide, rounded brow, radiated in the semi-darkness, "you are beautiful, you are beautiful . . . ."

When you would come back from the office, she was for you, a haven where you would be able to relieve your fatigue away from the noise and the traffic, and, she would cling to you, she would knot the charm, the grace of her arms around your neck: "good evening."

She would keep her apron on. You would sit down at the table in the kitchen. It felt good. The window panes, and even the glasses, the plates, the spoons, the forks, the knives were fogged up, because of the steam rising from the pots and the dutch oven on the stove.

What you both liked to eat, at the meals, were the grayish crusts, the clayey yellowish, the pockets of fine dark ashes, the bulgings, the excavations, the blackish deposits with white peaks, the loose or compact ground, the conjugated effects of salt and wind on the surface, and you would use your molars to ingest these partially cooked or partially rid of dirt and sand foods,

to try voraciously to return to the irrigable, waterable, producing soil,

which undulates, which puckers, which slopes,

to the sweetness of its valleys, of its shelves, of its hills, of its plains,

to the tones of its wheat wavy, zony, under the sun burning without consuming itself,

to the earth which supports us.

"You, you're a woman from around here...." "Then you would both enter the bedroom.

Here she is, warmth, stark naked, the sacs of her breasts would abound in flesh soft to caress, to kiss, through which showed the combustion of the pulmonary breathing, the spongy of her lobules, of her alveolae imbued with life, against which you would warm yourself, which you would squeeze so tight, so tight, oh! no! you will not be torn from her.

Here she is, this baby-fat passivity, chubby, who did not even see you anymore, she was feeling you so, and yet she was staring at you with her large eyes,

"My peach skin . . . " and the light pink of her cheeks would vanish under your lips enough to let you kiss the immaterial, her motherhood, the goodness of her nature, so as no longer to be isolated by anything, not even by the skin, you were so closely mingled with this internal blood, with this face, with this body.

And often, you would say to yourself: "how does anyone dare kill?"

And under the sheet, you would sniff her, would aspirate a woman's emanations, the musty, this bacterial environment, these whiffs of excrement, of intimate hygiene and of perspiring flesh which did not bother you, this innerthigh of quiverings, this skin which, so easily, becomes chafed, smooth all the way to the toes; and that was she.

"I need you." You would reassure the physiological processes, her blondeness, the sebum of her beautiful clean hair, her proportions, her limbs, her bust, her bony frame softened by the plumpness, and you would not release your hold, and her being would enter through your nostrils, like pure air, "I won't leave you by yourself." You promised you would help her, you would fulfill her, even though, you also, in infinity, you occupied an objectively, unimportant place... "We have to believe in something, we have to believe in us... " and you would intermingle, you would interweave from a same need of human warmth.

Time, marked by the sun and by the moon, would pass ... would eventually replace you with your children ...

Lying on her side, tract vaguely sickening, almost bestial, of conception, she would gape.

Your nose characterized by an extreme development: she desired you.

The strong musculation of your neck: she desired you.

Your large shoulders and thorax: she desired you.

The erection of your penis powerful enough to perforate: she desired you.

Flanked against you.

Oh! her king so rough! oh! your bravery! her champion! similar to a boar, to a horse, to a ram, to a bull charging, male, throwing with hooves, the dirt, in swirls.

You would transfuse each other, bands, of gold, of blood types, RH positive and B, sexes married to the point of orgasm,

mix of interwoven fingers, legs, ankles, arms, wrists, where the individual forgotten in the bisexual monster, polycephalus of love, reaches the sacred, where all the genera of love achieve disinterest, abnegation, in order to fuse, to commune, to give a heart to life on earth, to the vegetables, to the gases, to water, to the rocks, to the animals, to men, to this whole where energies become entwined, become joined, and become harmonized with limitlessness: "my darling, my love, my love . . . "

You would bend her, you would mould her, she was proud that each breast was large, that your appetites had become infatuated with her, and, in the heart of the muslin, the overhang of her breasts would work the transparent blouse, would support the moves and the falls of the pleats, and, without losing anything of its projection, would be absorbed by the fabric whose whiteness was caused by it and which returned the surge of milk whose silky ascent you would rumple "you are so feminine, so feminine."

Her skin, in relation to the liquid element, would culminate, alleluias full of vitamins, emulsified by the suckling, the twin, comestible spheres, the breasts would hang down on her chest, were a part of her percentage of fat, she would spurt, this corpulent woman you were in love with, whom your hands, your lips pressed, with ardor, the best.

And you would lower the elastic of her slip, of her pants, down to her genital organs, while staring at her, while elevating her on the cosmic scale, as though she no longer had either a beginning or an end, as though she were the current of beings and things, that which carries us away, through life and death, toward an unknown destination, and you would move about on her surfaces at times bulging, at times flat, but always as chubby.

Even her joints, you would admire.

Her right shoulder, scarred by the smallpox vaccination.

"My darling . . . ." This human life . . .

The incarnadine vapors framed the alcoves; you would look at her prettiness, manor hostess where darkness would give off light.

And you would feel like genuflecting before this lady in the white dress clothéd, before this virgin and child, spangled with jewels, crowned with roses, before this portrait vignetted by the waves and by the moiré of her unbraided hair under the lace veil reaching her waist, before these bands of white lace applied to transparent fleshy beige, before these long lace angel-sleeves, before the shimmering effects of the princess stitch, of the tulle sequined with gold, before these lace engagings, before these nettings inlaid with Irish lace, before these muslin puffs . . .

And you would travel through the loose sheaves, the ricks of sewn twigs, the irregularity of interwoven threads, the gnarled, the cellulose, the finishing of the linen, the bundles of bark liber, the cylindrical filaments of the flax, the vegetable dress, in the process, under your caresses, of absorbing the sweat of her body, the sun rays, of being traveled over by the carbonic anhydride, by the steam, by the air,

and your fingernails would get caught on the embroidery of the contours, on the raised petal motifs, on the hoops, in the lozenges, on the bows, on the double-bows, on the roses, on the slabs, on the chain-stitches, on the openstitches, would lose themselves in the interweaving of the threads, in the netting of the lace, in the Venetian lace, in the Renaissance lace, in the fine Irish lace,

and you would dip in the sauce of her belly like that of a good milkmaid, you would knock on her skin, on the milk doors, you knew her to be close to instinct, careful to avoid harming the digestive functions, to protect your stomach, your intestines and she would invite you to eat hearty, at the copious mixture of foods that were the caseins, the rennet she would produce by drawing from her blood; she was rich, energetic and she would wheel the feel, the flesh, you would handle her teats gently, she would treat you well, and the juice, at the bottom of the crevices of flesh, would run, substance of each gulp, of each bite, of what there is that is stirring, variable, precious, banal, in a human being, of what, as she grew older, would make of her a good woman with a charitable body, apt to liberate, in order to comfort it, your persistence, your secret nostalgia, to be devoted, to render help, to suckle like, then, an old wet-nurse, like an old nanny, like a security closing and embracing, white from which you would see the horizon, the clouds, dawn.

And with all your thirst, with all your hunger for tenderness, you would vibrate, you would call for more . . .

This buttery chest tasting like hazelnuts that you would grab by the fistful: lactase, lactose, galactose and the mass of each breast separating from agitation like curdled milk, and these emulsion-eddies in the serum where the ferments were multiplying, milk with large fat globules, rolled up in balls, shaped in mounds, in mushes of butter, and this cremini of flesh,

and, in good health, nitrous, pleasant, larded with fat, not deceiving you about her nature, she would withstand the tooth, when, choosing the center of the piece, in the thick of the chest, you would bite

the needle lace, the bobbin lace, the whip-stitches containing her bust and her organs

and before reaching the granularity of the two breasts, you would dance at a ball of ruffles, of furbelows, of garters, of whalebones, of fasteners, of batiste, of pleats, of garlands, of stripes, of gathers, of slip knots, of fribble, of embroideries, of ribbons, of seams where,

impatiently, you would try to unlace, to unfasten, to unbutton,

where perspiration, with wear, had hardened the fabric,

where, feminiform, the flesh overflowed,

naked, beautiful bosom held in its normal position by your caresses like by the brassiere, and extensible, you would encircle it, you would adjust it, all the while allowing ease of sighing, of swelling even more,

"here you are, you would repeat, here you are . . . ," "here you are," "here you are," "here you are," "here you are," "finally! . . ."

and you would touch her through the embroidery with the well-padded design filled with close stitches, through each polka dot with satin stitches, through backstitches looped one into the other, through the good-virgin stitch, through the grain stitch, through the Marie-Antoinette stitch, through the layers of embroidering cotton-thread, through the thickness of the stuffing, through the mercerized raised surface padding her skin;

and your fingers would go through the material so as to better handle the squeezing of her breasts which, firm, would resist the hand, without acting as a spring,

and the act of moving your tongue, and the temperature of the membranes of your mouth would moisten this bosom felted by the nightgown lace like cheese by molds,

fat soufflé, stuffing, muffin,

dough extra-fat, as white as the organdy of a first communion:

"River of final remedy which rises from misery, restores innocence, cleanses he who wants to be saved, is it season, yet, to be your fruit?" Oh, direct contact with the truth of her skin! Oh, searching! Oh, redemptor! Oh, unsullied savor! Oh, filiation! Ave Maria! There is nothing blunted . . .

The skin which burns in the sun like silk . . .

You would bear down on the stretched material of the girdle, two cream jars with which she prepared each breast, and at the surface of her body, on the grid of trebles, on the latticed square, on the rows of stitches, of semi-trebles, of the crochet work which clothed her . . .

And under that, alive, the relic of her heart was beating . . .

And here is her smile where shine the lipgloss and the cheeks that your kisses butterskim . . .

daintier than a powder puff . . .

And the brocade of her dress rustles with golden panniers, the metals have furnished the fibers, and concocted a garden of fragrant coltsfoot, of eupatorium, of ageratum and of mignonette . . .

But now agitated, her belly similar to an egg, lets out a gurgling sound, under the red of the draping,

she walks, spun in silver

lady of quality,

you breathe her in while assimilating her desirable ash-blond hair into your blood,

beautiful wench, the one, this piece of meat, whose bellyful still in a state of soft dough, comes out as a milky juice under the pressure of the fingernail, and where you fashion tenderness from the bulk of the content with both hands by compressing thoroughly her belly, thoroughly her breasts, as though you wanted to make the excess of the juice of life they contain spurt

and where your hand slides flat, in the direction of the veiny current,

on the breasts tightly tied between strings rendering them "swell,"

and on the fat lard covering the complete kidney;

then you dig your fingers into the hollows and the folds of the pink skin, into the muscles where her fat favorably rivals with butter,

and you savor, with smackings,

and the toasting was juicy, rich, savory, stout, stuffed tongue, candied flowers, assorted tarts, relisheries, pampano, porringer, hungerbuster, ullage, allium, calabash, terrapin, leveret, pink bottom stew, crullers, curds, crumpets, clabber, loquat, kumquat, pandowdy, cock-a-leekie, piccalilli, redfin, butterscotch, pawpaws, popovers, buttered cabbage hearts, pruinose, dumplings, skewers of longnecks, maids of honor, Brown Betty, botargo, bergamot, battelmat, tidbits, cowberries, yam, forcemeat, chitterlings, nettle soup, cracklings, fritters, saucials, pumpkinette, prickle pears, of a pantry,

would produce the strength to work, to walk, to talk, the heat which prevents the body's cooling,

you would grope her, you would snuggle there, you would coddle yourself there,

would lift her second ruffled slip of crepe de Chine, of Pompadour silk, fluted, edged with Valenciennes and with Paris stitching,

but more and more, she would be piping, scalloping, puckering, padding, upholstering herself,

basting cotton, threads, thread ribbons, percale ribbons, twilled ribbons, cotton ribbons, loose ribbons, ribbon in a bow, bias binding, braiding,

would become ornamented with eyelets, rosettes,

would expand in you, would invade you; would overtake your touch, your taste, your vision, your olfaction, your nervous system,

and would look, like a quest, like the nostalgic need which, from birth to death, would not have left you, and which, after death, would survive you maybe . . .

The thread, now, would seem to be coming out of her as though she had spinning nipples, as though she had silk glands, to be threading itself through the eye of a needle, and the needle and thread would pass, pass again through the chain threads, and would cross them, reinforcing the faded Brussels tulle, would pass over the trebles, over the meshes, and would be heading for another stitch, and would turn, would form the thickness of each loop, would double, triple itself, would sew through the row of braid, would pass through the thread loops, would tighten the whipstitches, would tighten the bows, would give more firmness to the edges, would work in as much thread as the tulle meshes could contain, and would embroider on her, enhancing her white carnation,

and you would watch the passing of the threads, through transparency, luxuriating in this mellowness, in this deshabille, in these frivolities, duchess lace, Venetian point, Cluny lace, Flanders lace, Bruges lace, Colbert lace,

and without twisting, you would squeeze the fripperies with your hands, then you would dive with them into the warm and soapy water,

then you would rinse them, in order to eliminate the soap, then delicately, you would lay them on several layers of clothes . . .

English lace, Brabant lace, Mirecourt lace, Bayeux lace, Chantilly lace,

which on her skin, would form these rosettes, these stars, these wheels, these arcs, these lozenges,

and would connect the designs with openstitches.

The man and the woman would embrace each other; she would be cast against him, against the dapplegray coat, against the napping whose flakes, whose asperities would scratch her face a little, against this sort of textile emanation of the muscular, patient man, where a refuge could be sought, and, just by being at the threshold of the body, just by making this contact, she would already feel her own existence being reinforced with another existence . . .

You would bare her neck; the thread, on each of the loops of the long dress were entwined like sunshine; you would caress the cuffs, the blouse whose net embroidery would indicate the fleshiest part; you would linger on the links in the shape of lozenges, on the ribbed rosettes of the chest.

She would lift her eyes modulated by the glare, toward you.

You would inhale her. An aroma of violet, of cassia, and of iris, the scent of her soap would emanate from her, from her loose hair,

from this lace embroidered muslin which haloed her, near the tulle curtains softening the too bright light;

you would froth her.

You would stuff her, so as to add a lot of embossment.

You would fluff her, would pulp her, would encrust your hands in the white, would wrinkle the padding of the motifs, the fillings of thick cotton, while trying to slip your fingers into the little circles, into the little cut-out leaves and under the thread straps, in order to feel the skin, the breast tips.

She would quiver, crotch, underarms of costly lace, would hide, from the waist, in yards of width, in the fullness.

Flocculent with ribbons.

You would listen to the swishing, the whistling of her petticoats, of her apron.

You would coddle, dandle, fondle the buckram girdling her. The creasings, the bridges of the lace. You would pull the zipper. Her breasts half bare, would react friskily, would overflow all around your hands. Roly-poly. But their nudity still appearing through the filter of a gauze. Mammillae in fritter, frisky, frizzled, fraternizing, are having a feast, a fricassee of good warm milk, engulfed in ruffles lustrous from ironing, in the kinks, in the ribbons, in the pleatings, in the ruches,

"my pretty one . . . ."

She was pretty: like the wheat when it goes to straw and goes to seed, like the delicate green knots of young wheat, like wheat a little tall already, in stalks, like the poppies, the cornflowers, the thistles, like wild oats vying with the wheat for air, water and fertilizer: like a soil well rested for sowing, like the Beauce region, in the Eure-et-Loire, well cultivated region, meadow of mowed crop, land for grains having given precious taste and nutritious qualities to her peasant blood . . .

And under the rococo bouquets painted with transparent colors, you would touch all sides of the member, the good steady veins, the veins at the fold of the elbow, the beatings of the arteries, the large veins with thick walls, the veiny crossroad, the skin covering the veins... But the means for a transfusion? to inject yourself in her, to pass through the circulatory torrent? to be taken out of your discomfort in order to know only her, only her softness, much dearer to your heart than your life? . .

"You are so devoted! so healthy!
Have mercy!
Have mercy!
Have mercy!
Listen
Grant my wish
Have mercy!
Have mercy!
Guide

Feed
Heal
Protect
me!
Reconcile me with truth!
Bring me back to truth!"

She would glow with garnets, with bloodstone, with sapphirine, with this vividness of blood.

You would look at her, she would realize that it was no longer she you were seeing, that it was no longer she you were addressing . . . that she was opening a path for you, that she was diversifying, that she was overdigging depressions where meanders would unfold and would become embanked in masses of love with dimensions unsuspected . . .

You would pursue your quest where the sun, at the heart of her blondeness, was never hot enough to dispel the mists, the dew, similar to those remnants of old fragile silk set on a layer of golden tulle.

And the sunlight in the attic room would emit some silk, would become covered with a netting of silk threads; the shimmers would drift, leaving behind them, threads settling here and there, would spin the center, the rays, the frame which the rising currents of the warm air would take away vertically, would stretch into threads ever longer, more golden, which would fuse to form this cloth almost intangible like the gossamers caught in the trees, in the plants of a forest,

in order to veil the smallness of your body . . .

And there, protected, far from shocks, you loved untying, retying her long hair, caressing her legs sheathed in silk stockings (she was, under the double ruffles, unctuous, extra-fat to please), curling up in her sleeves divided in three puffs by rows of pearls, penetrating her farthingale, the satin in two shades of pink, the taffetas, the fluted lace ruff, the ruffled cretonne, "my fairy . . . "

polyglobulic, rich in lucocytes, in hormones and mineral salts like placenta bathing the villosities. And she would concentrate. The umbilical beatings had not ceased. You would both agglomerate, you would form some sort of accumulation, of agglomerates that the brewing would render more voluminous still.

The red corpuscles would breathe, would settle the oxygen while you were embracing, while you were kissing, "stay near me, stay near me, oh! stay near me! . . . " while you were led from yourself to her and brought back from her to yourself, without interruption in a movement of vital maintenance where an exchange of your bloods was being made . . .

And the walls were draped with crimson damask, the blood was on the move and the shadows, the alcove would turn red, would absorb the vermilion, the scarlet, most of the brocade's reds, and would become deeper with the weight and with the matter of the reds and the coloring substance, under the brightness of the fabric, would flood the depth of the background, would serve as your shelter, and the interferences of the light, at the surface of the audacious neckline, would tan her, would bronze her, would silver her, would gild her, passing on to her the metallic appearance of the red brocade of this dress glistening; the shimmering play of light radiating through the atmosphere of the room would gleam, on the bulging of her breasts, modifying them like a super-light that you could caress; the peripheral color reactions were created by the extreme luminosity of the flesh and of the blue of the veins which showed through the skin, at the golden center. And her presence would emerge from the reddening fusion of the light with the shadows where, on your knees, in front of her, you would pray . . .

She was wearing a vest laden with golden floriations . . .

The young woman, in a short dress, gets up from the bed to make a phone call, in the next room . . .

You were dreaming her . . .

She would keep intensifying as, in the velvet, you would penetrate.

You are trying to come closer to the origin; you sense the urgency of turning back, of slowing the future, the race toward the end, you are afraid; the threshold of degradation has been reached, life empties itself of life . . . cities, machines, concentrationary giantism gnaw on the earth, the sea, the sky . . . the species . . .

Her lids closed from pleasure: it was marvelously soft, like touching a rose; your reflection was mirrored in it, you would see your own glance become more defined on the swarthiness, on the little wrinkles, on the delicate graininess of the shimmering eyelids. Their skin was pinkish on top, more or less tinged with mauve and purple underneath, would vary from pure white to the violet purple of the capillary vessels, you would contemplate these pigments which would fade after death . . .

Lower, above her belt, your hands would mould the curvaceous shape of her bosom enhanced, illuminated by the mixture of gold threads and silver threads, by the solid gold appareling her, setting her like a diamond, causing her to dazzle, causing her to cast sparkles like a treasure, as though her glands were secreting luminous energy . . .

And you would anoint with oil, you would massage the still tender skin of her skull at the ash-blond hairline, the frizzes, the down surrounding the bulbous brow . . .

And the texture of her skin was so delicate that it was barely perceptible under your fingers . . .

And she would lead you to the interior of the lands where would shine, Grace!

in the summer, dog days, like spangles around the house solidly set in the silt of the plain, in the fields . . .

Fecundity of the World!

You were hungry for density, to physically feel the epiderms, the material reality, the weight and matter of objects, with the triviality, with the gluttony of the mouth and the hands.

wide bellied smoked ham, small town butcher shop: its automatic scales, its grinders, its cleavers, its saws, its refrigerated displays, bakehouse, everything would seem so good to your organs and hers, would melt into the hazy texture of this cosmic generosity, of this dough that it is the responsibility of a human being to knead, to preserve and to develop with adoration . . .

Your penis, ass-tickler, you had it hard, you had it mad, you had it high, you had it in erection for this wheat . . .

Sanctus. Sanctus. Sanctus.

But may your innocence, may your Faith stay the Child.

The lettuces, the spinach, the cabbages, over acres, would transpire gallons of water, would exhale millions of pounds of steam.

You would devoutly place your lips on the grooves, on the tits, on the mounts, on the valleys, on the gorges, on the creeks, on the handles, on the escarpments, on the foot-hills, on the plateau of the crop-producing land . . .

While the womb, while its involuntary and convulsive contractions, would moan, was seeded, under you, and that months later, she would give life, while the innersprings of the mattress would squeak, in the bedroom.

and Joy!

Joy!

Joy!

The coleaptera's elytrons, their nervation, the celestial blue, the iridescences of the open window on the harvest would become super-imposed on this cloud of lace and muslin where summer, where the hair and the golden coronets, shot through with daylight, would cascade to the floor.

Her chest, her belly with a navel like a dimple, her hips, without retaining their impression, would push back the fingers you would dig into them, she contained fragments of bran, was redolent, flesh for heavy hand kneading, from the last kneading. Your work, your sweat, in the kneading-trough, succeeded in swelling still more this so easily kneaded dough, you would allow her to blossom out, she would present a large, full breast, you would mould in the full flesh, in the fat of the contour, in the life of the flesh, in the mass . . .

But she would lose, if you abandoned her, her measurements, this fat like the land deprived of fertilizer becomes exhausted, dries up . . .

I love you!

I love you!

In spite of you,

In spite of me.

In spite of what will forever deprive me of you.

In spite of illness.

In spite of death.

In spite of decay . . .

And you are eternal!

You are eternal!

You are eternal!

In spite of the past.

In spite of the present.

In spite of the future.

In spite of time.

You are in my love you are eternal you are eternal.

You are in my thirst!

You are in my hunger!

And as her presence would spread, not a single human being, thanks to her, was unknown to you anymore, was a stranger to you anymore, she would become transfigured, would become generalized, would bring you closer to each organism, would reinstate universal kinship, you loved her so . . .

But misery, injustice, deprive you of a face, of a body, of youth, steal us from your arms, you remain nonetheless an emotion, a feeling, a vibration in our weeping heart, and your face is numberless like your arms, like life's products, in order to sensitize us, in order to teach us to love, to save.

Threadings, flowings of red in the process of setting off her body: the girdle would accentuate her plumpness whose buttocks, breasts, your hands would follow at length . . . She would lift with her hand the shimmering taffetas of her long dress to facilitate her walk, and would become lined in red and would be translated into cloth, would enter the silk fabric categories, would weave the chain of one red with the woof of another red, would melt her nuances one into the other, would become iridescent, would create new shapes, would radiate, would come back to her departure point, to this body offering a series of undulations, of waves, of circles caused by the light reflecting on the red dress, would make into clothes, the thickness, the substance of the silk fabric, and would coagulate, and would succeed, with the tinting, in producing a well- oxygenated red, in copying the iridescences of the blood,

and would reduce herself to designs of reddish flowers and would dawdle, balancing the rows of hoops in her panniers, under the flowered skirt, under the red taffetas trailing a yard long on the ground,

would pass by, would live, would die, would relive . . .

and would lean against the wall, red corpuscles, profile, silhouette . . . As though, however, she would always elude you . . .

Afterword

By Monique F. Nagem

Chantal Chawaf, whose literary accomplishments have yet to receive the attention due them in the United States, is the author of many compellingly lyrical novels which, since 1974, have been critically acclaimed in France. Chawaf's name usually comes up when discussion of other French feminist writers occurs, writers like Hélène Cixous or Monique Wittig. However, it cannot be said that Chawaf fits into their category precisely. Chawaf's literary corpus is more than a feminine lexical experiment, more than a practice of writing which inscribes the female body and female difference in language and text. It is a joyous celebration of the body; it is a quest for the peaceful reunion of the body and the spirit; it is an anguished cry for understanding and love between men and women; it is a conscious exploration of the mother-daughter bond; it is a rejoicing in the erotic pleasures of the female body and the beauty of the woman, in images resonant with mystical and mythical echoes of pre-patriarchal times. According to Chawaf the lack of balance in human relations (that is, relations between men and women) is caused by a lack of verbal language of the feminine. This language is the product of a passion which supersedes sexual fusion; it is the product of symbolic fusion, and it is through the latter that men and women divest themselves of their fear of the feminine, of the body, of the mother, of the other, of woman.

Mothering and motherhood, the pains and the joys of giving birth or being given birth is one of the prevalent themes of Chawaf's novels. In *Mother Love*, a young woman tries to recreate, in words and images, the mother who died at her birth. *Chair Chaude* [*Warm Flesh*] (1976) is a loving dialogue between a mother and her daughter. *Cercoeur* [*Graveheart*] (1976) deals with the anguish of losing a child. In *Le Soleil et la Terre* [*The Sun and the Earth*] (1977) Chawaf opposes man's inevitable need to wage war to the love of a mother for her daughter and the mother's need to protect that daughter. *Crépusculaires* [*Crepusculars*] (1981) is an interesting shift from the mother-daughter relationship to the dynamics between a father and a daughter.

The other major theme of Chawaf's novels is the relationship between men and women. In *Mother Earth* the emphasis is on sexual love from the woman's point of view. In *Les Landes* (1980), a woman in the solitude of the windswept coast of southwestern France, tries to make sense of a failed love affair. In *La Vallée incarnate* [*Incarnadine Valley*] (1984), a man and a woman share in the happy anticipation of parenthood and through their love for each other achieve peace and freedom. In her latest novel *Rédemption* [*Redemption*] (1989), the man is a vampiric killer of women who is brought to redemption through the intercession of a woman.

All these novels are fed by a voice that enunciates the narrative in an elaborate, stream-of-consciousness style that reaches deep into the labyrinth of human emotions. Syntax is often disrupted; conventional sentence structure is fragmented; Chawaf creates unconventional patterns of logic; she mixes registers of speech (even languages as in *Redemption*); sometimes she uproots words from their customary beds and replants them to let them blossom in unfamiliar surroundings. Temporal continuity and cause and effect, the components of a conventional narrative, are replaced by a flow of words or phrases which produces a rhythm replicating the surge of birth or the hypnotic drive of violence. These novels seldom have an authoritative narrator to reassure the reader of the "truth" of the narrative; the voice often asks questions to which there do not always seem to be readily available answers.

The present text, *Mother Love, Mother Earth* (originally titled *Retable, La Rêverie* in French) is a very early novel (1974) that introduces many of Chawaf's major themes. The title *Mother Love, Mother Earth* unites two texts which, though separate, form a diptych, each panel of which is the recreation of the invention of experience from loosely connected bits and pieces of information. The first panel is a dysphoric text introducing many of the themes which recur in later Chawaf novels, such as the cathexis between a mother and a daughter, the opposition of city and technology to nature and crafts, and the devastation of war. The other panel is a euphoric reverie set in some remote past in a space of harmony.

Mother Love, the first panel, is a dramatic rendition of a death and a birth. The birth is that of Ghyslaine; the death, that of her mother. Ghyslaine had been led to believe by her adoptive parents that her mother, possibly a prostitute, or at any rate a woman of loose morals, had given her up for adoption. She finds out, however, that her mother and father, both university professors, were in fact killed in a bombing raid in 1944, just as the mother was about to give birth. The baby was saved by a Caesarian operation. The twenty-five-year old Ghyslaine, with the few facts she has about her mother, attempts to re-create her own conception, her painful birth and the death of her mother, through fantasy. This unknown past is recovered not with descriptions, but by means of verbal constructs that push language to its outer limits. The imaginary rendition of Ghyslaine's birth becomes a paradigm for the birth of a narrative, which, like an actual birth, is difficult, messy, and at times violent; it is a birth out of a void. When the narrative voice begins the section titled "Portrait," it takes stock of what has been narrated so far, then decides to "tackle this differently. . . ." It recapitulates the scraps of information available.

The French title *Retable* is the name of a type of altarpiece typical of the Renaissance, sumptuously decorated, generally incorporating painting and sculpture. It is usually a group of hinged panels, arranged so the outer sections fold over the inner ones. Chawaf's text is structured to resemble the Renaissance artifact; like a retable, it is made up of panels, three in this case, whose main subject appears on the inner panel while related subjects appear on the outer panels. In addition, the religious connotations of the title are echoed repeatedly in the text, culminating in a portrait of the mother carrying the child:

At the parochial crossroads of the bosom and the arms, the breathing flushes the host, protects its warmth, dandles in the wet gold of the swaddling clothes, of the sheets, of the pillow, of the baptismal dress and of the diaper, this is where tenderness, relic and transmitted through the sensitive tips of skin, burns like a taper between the ovoli of the gallery and the liturgical embroidery of the support bows.

Mortuary chapel.

The first panel of the diptych, *Mother Love*, ends with a question which the second panel, *Mother Love*, answers. *Mother Earth* is, however, life following destruction, sexual love following sacred mother love, and, like its companion piece, it is just as much an imaginary rendition, this time of the love between a man and a woman. The couple could be Ghyslaine's parents, but they are more; they take on universal dimensions and become a paradigm for male-female relations.

In both *Mother Love* and *Mother Earth*, Chawaf achieves meaning in a variety of ways, most of which contribute to the uncanny quality of the texts whose process it is necessary to retrace in order to arrive at understanding. From the first, Chawaf establishes semantic fields which she then intermingles to create unconventional patterns of logical meaning; she challenges the reader's expectations by transgressing semantic and syntactic rules. As a narrative, therefore, the novel transgresses certain literary rules of conventional narration, forcing the reader to reconstruct Ghyslaine's story by retracing the different semantic fields of the text. There is no authoritative voice to reassure the reader of the "truth" of Ghyslaine's erratic narration. The only narrative frames in *Mother Love* are the section headings I "Birth," II "Portrait," III "Mausoleum." As part of the "Birth" narrative, there is a subsection entitled "Document," a heading which is given authority with a footnote (the only one in the text) revealing that this is a "record of events which have really happened." The reader presumes that this section reveals the truth that Ghyslaine's parents had been hiding. *Mother Earth*, on the other hand, is not even framed by section titles; it is simply divided into parts of unequal length.

Chawaf also performs her own linguistic revolution. She derails the sentence in numerous ways; she reverses the usual order of words; sometimes she begins a sentence with verbs whose subject finally surfaces a few lines later. She assigns to nouns the function of verbs or vice-versa; she renders intransitive verbs transitive. Chawaf has stated that she never pre-organizes or calculates her work; it simply organizes itself. The end result is not as casual as that statement might make it seem. Like the French Renaissance poets of *La Pléiade*, who wanted to renew the French language by using words drawn from technical vocabularies, Chawaf incorporates words as diverse as medical terms, words referring to geological formations, architectural terms, a variety of sewing terms and names of different types of lace, some more obscure than others. By so doing she achieves a variety of effects. She establishes semantic fields or reinforces those she has already introduced, she rejoices and invites the reader to rejoice in the materiality of words, and she opens her text to plurisignificance.

In addition to releasing a multitude of words like a flower its pollen, Chawaf manipulates words in order to sustain multiple levels of meaning. Like Lewis Carroll's lithe and slimy "slithy" or James Joyce's "yung and easily freudened" girls, Chawaf's "Scatstrecherize" a *portmanteau* word, enriches the text by combining "scatter" and "stretch." Some of Chawaf's neologisms derive their plurisignificance from their musical or tonic quality and as in the case of *blondoyer*, from the multitude of connotations they evoke. One of the few facts Ghyslaine has about her mother is that she was blonde; that epithet therefore is not only incorporated in the young woman's imaginary recreations of her mother, but the image of blondeness is dispersed throughout the text. "Blonde" triggers a series of associations. As is already known, Ghyslaine's mother is from the North, she is tall and slender; she is often associated with those aspects of nature which are blonde or yellow like the sun, wheat, and daffodils; like the sun her warmth radiates any room she occupies in Ghyslaine's imagination. Her blondeness also symbolizes her ethereal, dreamlike qualities and inaccessibility. The verb Chawaf created, *blondoyer*, is used to describe what the mother's hair does, as one might write that hair shines or undulates, and in another instance it is used to refer to what the mother does under the sycamores, as one might write that a person radiantly strolls about. One of the functions of the verb is to allude to the mother; another is to evoke the liquid properties already associated with mother and the birth of Ghyslaine with the "i" sound, a phonetically liquid consonant in French, reinforced by the muted "on," and by its resemblance to a French verb ending in "oyer" (of which there are very few in French), *ondoyer*, which means to undulate or ripple as would waves. A third function of the verb, in the second instance, is to rhyme with *tournoyer* [to twirl] which appears earlier in the sentence.

Many of the words which Chawaf creates in the novel have an agrarian motif, recapitulating the myth of the Great Earth Mother with her variants. The flesh of the woman in both *Mother Love* and *Mother*

Earth is often identified with soil, loam, or clay. In *Mother Love,* Ghyslaine desperately attempts to recreate her mother's native earth from the minimum of information she has. The imagined mother was blonde like a wheat rose. The woman in *Mother Earth* is also compared to wheat. Nature, which abounds in both texts, is always bountiful, shady, cool, and damp. There are no carnations in her world but many daffodils and alfalfa, flowers which grow naturally. The country of origin of the woman in *Mother Earth* is the Beauce region, the bread-basket of France. The man who makes love to her calls her a country woman, a woman from these parts [*une femme du pays*]. The kitchen activities of the woman often relate to milk and its products; by the same token the semantic field of dairy products profusely evokes the beauty of the woman. Ghyslaine's ideal re-creation of her mother includes the moments before birth, strongly reminiscent of the ancient ritual of giving birth upon the soil associated with the Great Earth Mother.

> It is raining on the seaweeds, in the middle of the road rays of sky, shining, fullness of apricot, in front of the sprinkled border and the woman facing into the wind, resins right in the hay and the placenta of the meadow, right in the chirping of the elytrons, right in the sandy bottoms of the ovaries, it still seated on the ground ready to give birth; she bathes, in the heart of the trees, her breast like milk seaweeds, among the strawberries and permeates.

The first half of the diptych *Mother Love, Mother Earth* ends with the question, "What did we do to lose the savor of the earth-mother?" The voice in the text suggests as an answer, "But let us move on toward her! so we can at last be allowed to love, to cross over to the zone of love. . ." In *Mother Earth* the zone of love is deployed and the love-fusion of the man and the woman take on mythical echoes. The woman becomes a bounty of adipose flesh. The man making love to her revels in her rolls of fat, in her enormous breasts liberated from their castigating prisons and swelling under his touch. She is the Great Earth Mother. This union, however, occurs in a Utopian world set in some immemorial past. Since the goal is unattainable, *Mother Earth* ends with the fear that the feminine side of man will always elude him. It is an imaginative creation, aided by language, that fires our energies and desires. Utopia only exists linguistically.

If a writer like Chawaf is to be properly evaluated in a literary world whose boundaries have become more relaxed with the years, her work must be translated for the benefit of interested readers whose knowledge of French is too spare, or non-existent, to read her in the original. Like Ghyslaine representing her absent mother, the translator represents an absent text, therefore the re-presentation is more likely to be much less fragmented than Ghyslaine's.

This translation of *Mother Love, Mother Earth* attempts to preserve a balance between the exact and the natural—that is, Chawaf's text is reproduced in all its uncanniness with, nevertheless, careful vigilance to avoid any extreme difficulties for the anglophone reader. Sometimes such a balance is unattainable; in that case, the translator has chosen to sacrifice naturalness rather than exactness. One such problem which recurs throughout the text is Chawaf's delight in using technical terms for various subjects from medicine to body parts to geology. French, a Romance language, is more tolerant of such formality than English, a Germanic language, since many technical terms are Latinate in derivation. For this reason some passages of Chawaf's texts run the risk of sounding pedantic. In spite of this risk, however, the more technical terms must be used to comply with the overall pattern in which they participate, a pattern made obvious by the fact that when there is a choice in French, Chawaf invariably chooses the rarer, or more obscure word.

In spite of these differences in attitude toward registers of language by speakers of the two languages, there are many similarities between French and English, the result of years of linguistic exchanges between the two cultures. The difficulties arise from Chawaf's morphological, semantic, syntactic, and structural distortions. Morphological distortions are rare in Chawaf's text, and they usually involve the doubling of a consonant as in the verb *barater*, which means to turn cream into butter, which she spells *barrater*. It is possible to render this distortion by adding and "r" to *butter*; yet such a transformation is much less subtle in English than it is in French. English orthographic rules do not produce such an ending. Therefore the distortion was not translated in the English language text. The semantic dilemmas, however, are much more numerous and are the result of prime differences in the two languages, as well as Chawaf's distortions. Neologisms, which already present a problem to the reader of the original text, constitute a special problem for the translator. Some of these can be taken apart in the source language, with their components translated into the target language and reconstituted to form equivalent neologisms, as in the *scatstrecherize* described earlier. *Feminiform* is the result of the same procedure. However a neologism like *joliveté*, a noun fabricated from an existing adjective, can only be rendered as *prettiness*, and as a result the distortion is lost.

Even without intended distortions, poetic language requires special attention if rhythms, sounds, and multiple connotations and resonances of words are to be replicated in the target language. Culture-bound words which are charged with meaning even in purely prosaic language are even more connotative in poetic language; in fact the author relies heavily on their allusions. Chawaf, who places the protagonist of *Mother Earth* in the Beauce region of France not only counts on its multiple echoes for the French reader, but also plays on the morphological ramifications of the word, which contains the adjective *beau* [beautiful] in its sound. Historical allusions can also represent a loss in the target language. In order to minimize these losses some translators favor the use of footnotes. In fact, Vladimir Nabokov, a bold innovator among translators, believed that the more footnotes the better. Other translators believe that footnotes are an encumbrance in a literary text. In *Mother Love*, Chawaf refers to *l'exode* (the exodus), which for any French reader immediately elicits images of Parisians fleeting their capital ahead of the advancing German army in 1940. To make such a word more temporally relevant to a reader of the English language text, for whom Biblical images would appear, it is translated as *the 1940 exodus*. The minimal added information does not interfere in the text and, at least, anchors the time reference for a non-French reader.

When a direct synonym for a word cannot be found in the target language, an equivalent is used. Some equivalents do not restrict the original intentions of the source text, such as *glou-glou* translated as *glug-glug* or *kilometres* changed to *miles*, and they make the translation more natural, but words abundant in connotations such as *passe-velours* [amarinthine] lose their impact when an equivalent is used. In *Mother Earth*, *passe-velours* appears in a series of words which suggest a shade of red, begin with a "p" and describe the woman's flesh positively. The word in English does not have the phonetic and lexical connotations of the softness of *velours* [velvet]; in addition, velvet belongs to the semantic field of sewing and embroidering prevalent in the text.

"Poppy," the word chosen as an equivalent, translates the alliterative sound and the color, but not the referent, nor does it belong to the same semantic field. *Aoûtement* is another charged word which, on the other hand, can be translated denotatively as "maturescence," but which then loses the agrarian echoes of harvest and the month of August, as well as the morphological connections to which another word which surfaces more than once later in the text, *ouate*, which means cotton wool.

Finally, because of the morphological closeness of some French and English words, certain sounds and even rhythms can be reproduced; however others cannot. The translator is at the mercy of the arbitrariness of the sign and must choose to reproduce either the semantic or the phonetic elements, but not both. In *Mother Love* the woman's vulva is described as "*poilue, potelée, potée*," a series smoothly rendered in English as "pilose, pottering, plump," but "Sparks. Wings. Eyelashes," loses the fluidity of "*Etincelles. Ailes. Cils.*" One passage in *Mother Earth* is a microcosm of translation problems encountered in a text such as Chawaf's. The French version,

> et la, rôtie était fondante, grasse, savoureuse, corsée, langue
> fourrée, fleurs confites, tartes trillées, pourlecheries, meurette,
> terrinée, matefaim, ouillade, aillade, cujassou, chaudrée,
> lapereau, fricandeau de mousserons, galouille, caillebottes,
> corgnottes, cancoillote, viquotte, rigotte, patissous, ballotines,
> mélusine, mogettes rouges, berlingolettes, galetons, poupetons,
> embeurée de choux pommes, prune, nouillettes, brochettes
> d'argouane, dianes, bourride, boutargue, béatilles, bigarde,
> bouillinade, vacherin, wam, farçon, rillons, tourin, gratons,
> bugne, sauciaux, citrouillet, poires pisserettes, d'un garde-man
> ger, . . .

is a compendium of neologisms, obscure words, and names of rare or regional dishes, pouring out in a series of phonetic and alliterative suggestions recalling the semantic fields associated with the woman. In order to preserve these semantic fields with their alliterations and assonances, the English version becomes not an exact word-for-denotative-word translation, but an equivalent litany of neologisms, obscure words, with the names of rare or regional dishes arranged in such a way as to reproduce similar alliterations and assonances:

> and the toasting was juicy, rich, savory, stout, stuffed,

tongue, candied flowers, assorted tarts, relisheries, pampano, porringer, hungerbuster, ullage, allium, calabash, terrapin, leveret, pink bottom stew, crullers, curds, crumpets, clabber, loquat,kumquat, pandowdy, cock-a-leekie, piccalilli, redfin, butterscotch, pawpaws, popovers, buttered cabbage hearts, pruinose, dumplings, skewers of longnecks, maids of honor, Brown Betty, botargo, bergamot, battelmat, tidbits, cowberries, yams, forcemeat, chitterings, nettle soup, craklings, fritters, saucials, pumpkinette, prickle pears, of a pantry, . . .

To arrive at an equivalent reproduction of the impression this passage gives in the French text, the translator resorted to reducing the litany to one-word units of translation, and in the case of some of these units, to one-morpheme units. Each French word was listed in one column; its denotative translation, if there was one, was arrived at with the help of the *Larousse Gastronomique* and various French cookbooks in another; and its phonetic peculiarities were listed in a third column. Then with the help of American cookbooks, the translator established a list of culinary nouns with phonetic attributes similar to those in the French list, and with denotations which fit the various food categories of the French terms, such as milk and cheese, fish, fruits, obscure regional names, or those which include the names of women, as is the case with two of the words in French.

In some instances the denotation happened to fill the linguistic and phonetic requirements of the translation as in *leveret* for *lapereau* or *botargo* for *boutargue*; in others a close equivalent was found, such as *prickle pears* for *poires pisserettes*; or *dumplings* for *nouillettes*. In the case of *caincoillotte*, the name of a specific type of cheese, *clabber*, a generic term, was used, a translation which keeps the image intact. Some of the French words are neologisms: *sauciaux* became *saucials* and *matefaim* became *hungerbuster*, both exact equivalents of the French. Other neologisms such as *corgniotte* and *viquotte* or *cujassou* and *galouille* were categorized as parts of the overall impression and were rendered in English with the names of foods whose sounds approximated the French sounds. Because some of the French names could be translated directly, such as *béatille* (which means "tidbits"), but whose phonetic qualities did not match, the denotative translation does not necessarily appear in the same order as in the French text. For this reason "galouille, caillebottes, corgniottes, cancoillotte, viquotte" became "crullers, curds, crumpets, loquat, kum-quat."

When French readers encounter the above-quoted passage, it is the linguistic exuberance, intertwined in a network of food images, which washes over them, accompanied by an enjoyment of the experience as though they were savoring a copious meal. The readers become lexical *gourmands*. The experience should be the same for the anglophone readers.

The task of translation is not restricted to the shift from one foreign language to another, but also to the shift from one world-view to another. In each case the emphasis is on communication for the sake of harmony and mutual benefit. The translation of *Retable, La Rêverie* into *Mother Love, Mother Earth* transforms an absence into a presence; Chawaf's translation of an abstract sign into a fruit of the subconscious that liberates men as well as women.

Some Titles in the Series

JAMES J. WILHELM

General Editor

1. Lars Ahlin, *Cinnamoncandy*.
   Translated from Swedish by Hanna Kalter Weiss.

2. *Anthology of Belgian Symbolist Poets*.
   Translated from French by Donald F. Friedman.

3. Ariosto, *Five Cantos*.
   Translated from Italian by Leslie Z. Morgan.

4. Enrique Medina, *Las Tumbas*. Translated from Spanish
   by David William Foster.

5. Antonio de Castro Alves, *The Major Abolitionist Poems*.
   Translated from Portuguese by Amy A. Peterson.

6. Li Cunbao, *The Wreath at the Foot of the Mountain*.
   Translated from Chinese by Chen Hanming and
   James O. Belcher.

7. Meïr Goldschmidt, *A Jew*.
   Translated from Danish by Kenneth Ober.

8. Árpád Göncz, *Plays and Other Writings*.
   Translated from Hungarian by Katharina and
   Christopher Wilson.